MW01194342

Romance Writing Prompts to Spark Your Imagination

By
Annette Elton

CreateSpace Edition

Cover design by Tatiana Vila – Vila Design

Copyright 2015 by Annette Elton All rights reserved.

License Notes

Visit my website at
http://www.makealivingwritingromance.com.

~~******~~

Table of Contents

~~******~~

Introduction - Getting Started

Writing a romantic story seems like such a simple concept. Two people meet. Something gets in their way or prevents them, temporarily, from getting together. They overcome it and live happily ever after.

Right?

On the surface, it's nothing more than telling a story, translating it from your imagination to the printed word.

Yet, as you may well know, it can be a complicated and frustrating process. Good story ideas are difficult to come by. And when you think you have a good story idea, what do you do with it? How do you turn it into a full romance novel with…

• A compelling hero and heroine (who aren't stereotypes, but are archetypes)?
• Interesting supporting characters (who don't steal the story, but make it more interesting)?
• Great dialogue
• Descriptive scenes
• Conflict
• Internal and external motivations
• Character growth
• And, oh yeah…a plot?

It's not as easy as it looks, but every good romance novel begins the same way – with a story idea.

How to Use this Book

The story starters in this book cover myriad genres, from erotic romance to inspirational and everything in between. You'll find there are also different types of story starters including dialogue starters, scenes and even story endings.

The story starters are meant to help kick start your imagination.

You can change ANYTHING about the story starter. Take the idea and bend it to your will – you're the boss.

Use the ideas to help you overcome writer's block.

It doesn't matter if you're staring at a blank page or if you're in the middle of a novel and unsure where to go with it – use the starters as inspiration. Let them help get your creative brain fired up.

Use the ideas to strengthen your writing muscles.

Your writing muscles are like any other muscle in your body. If you don't use them regularly, it becomes weak. Don't let your creative writing muscles atrophy! Even if you're not working on a story idea, write. Grab a story idea and fill a page or two (or ten) or write for twenty minutes – you make the rules.

A word of advice…Keep what you write.

Even if you don't use it in a story, keep what you write. It may come in handy tomorrow or ten years from now. I've written single scenes that turned into novels years later. You just never know when something small may turn into something tremendous. Don't let your ideas or your hard work get lost.

Extra Help

At the end of the book you'll find a link to my website.
Click on it and you'll be able to access free downloadable,
and printable, worksheets.

These worksheets cover everything from how to track
agent and editor submissions, to how to revise your
manuscript, to how to turn a story idea into a fully realized
novel.

They're free for the taking. Just click on the "Worksheets
and Downloads" page and download what you need.

And always feel free to contact me if you have any
questions or comments. My email is
info@makealivingwritingromance.com

~~*******~~

Chapter 1

Historical Romance, Time Travel

1. A woman is writing a book. It was inspired by a story her friend told her about her ancestors. To hold onto the inspiration she has some belongings of the real life hero, now dead.

He haunts her dreams and eventually her waking hours. He becomes her muse. Write about their first encounter. When does she realize he's not a figment of her imagination, but a real ghost?

2. An eye doctor is treating a beautiful blind patient. An accident caused her blindness and by all accounts she should be able to see. He decides to make her case his primary project. What happens?

3. Josie is used to men throwing themselves at her. As the headline singer at a nightclub they want the notoriety of sleeping with her.

This makes her damned choosey when it comes to men, so when she finally finds a man she's interested in why won't he give her the time of day?

4. Your heroine is a 1930's circus performer. Why is she in the circus? What drew her to it and what is her story?

5. Your heroine is a hideaway on a steamliner in the 1910's. She meets your hero who is a passenger, mechanic, another

stowaway etc on the steam liner. What happens? Why is she hiding on the ship?

6. Your heroine is a stripper in the 1940's (think Gypsy Rose Lee). She's also a spy for the Government. Now her government wants her dead. Who can she trust and why does she trust him?

7. Your hero is a wealthy Duke. He acquires a piece of property that contains a small farm and the lovely farmer's daughter.

She immediately becomes the object of his dreams and desires. Who is your heroine and how does she react when she learns the Duke is the new owner of her farm?

8. Your heroine owns an apothecary. A man enters her store on the night of the mystical moon. What does he want? (A good premise for the beginnings of a historical romance.)

9. Your heroine is paid by the rival of your hero to spy on him. She earns a job in his home/business. As she gets to know him she's torn between her conscience and her desperate need for the cash, but your hero is wise to her activities and turns the tables on her. What does he do to her to catch her in the act and how does she react?

10. Your hero and heroine meet during the historic gold rush in California. How do they meet and why are they searching for gold (beyond the obvious reason – they need a motivation other than a desire for money/greed)?

11. A ragtime dancer meets musician in the 1920's. Both are trying to escape their past, and are on the search for fame and fortune. One night, both down on their luck, they

stumble into each other outside a club. What happened to bring them together?

12. Your hero is hunting in the woods when he sees a woman off in the distance. What happens next?

13. Your heroine produces wine during prohibition. What does she do when a handsome police officer confronts her?

14. Your hero is a spy. He is injured and takes refuge in the home of a woman he's met. What he doesn't know is that she is working for his enemy. What happens when he finds out?

15. Your heroine is standing in the entrance of an old mansion. It's grim, dusty, and feels like a mausoleum. She thinks to herself, "It's the perfect place to hide a corpse." The owner, standing before her, smirks as if he can read her thoughts. What happens next?

16. Your heroine is on a horse. She's riding through the forest, the trees rushing past her in a blur. Where is she going?

17. Your heroine is a saloon dancer. A gunfight breaks out in the saloon and a man protects her by throwing her to the ground. What happens next?

18. Your heroine and her sister compete with each other on everything, including men. When your heroine finds "the one" she is bound and determined to keep him from meeting her sister. What happens?

19. Your heroine works in Florence Nightingale's house as a servant around the time that Florence is making her

decision to enter nursing. It inspires your heroine to make a big change in her life too. What is it?

20. Your hero is a playboy. He mistakes a woman for her twin, who is one of his frequent playmates. He didn't know she was a twin. When he takes the twin home he gets a big surprise. What happens?

21. Your heroine visits her friend for the weekend and captures the attention of the most powerful man in town. Why is he powerful? How do they meet?

22. Your heroine is a pirate. It's a man's world and she has to be tougher and more relentless than the others. She must make an example of the man she wants more than all the riches in the sea. What happens?

23. Your heroine is a matchmaker. She's great at helping others find love, and terrible at finding love for herself. After a particularly horrible date she meets him. How do they meet?

24. Your heroine gave her innocence to the one man she has always loved. She wakes in the morning to find he has vanished. Five years later he is back. What happened?

25. An artist is wounded and unable to paint/draw/sculpt or compose (you decide). Discouraged and frustrated, he/she hides away and is reawakened to the possibilities by whom?

26. Your heroine is a master at torture and is employed by the King to get secrets out of their prisoners. (You determine the time period and kingdom.) When she meets your hero she risks her life, and her heart, to help him escape.

27. Your heroine has a unique career for a woman during the Gold Rush – she's a blackjack dealer. When a player accuses her of cheating what happens?

28. Your bad boy hero returns to the town he grew up in and has to rely on a woman who thought she was too good for him. Why does he have to rely on her? Why is he back in town? What happens?

29. Your heroine was dumped by her boyfriend five years ago. His parting words were, "You're never going to be successful." She's now topped him on the richest people list and she's about to see him face to face for the first time since that day he dumped her. What does she say to him?

30. Your hero/heroine finds themselves shipwrecked. They think they are alone. Are they? Is someone on the island?

31. Your hero took off after a scandal. On the road for years, he wants to come home and clear his name. He needs the help of your heroine – a woman with the means to give him the legitimacy he desires. What did he do or what was he accused of and how does he convince your heroine to help him?

32. Your heroine is captured by Indians. She falls for one of the tribe members. When they release her, she must decide whether to stay or to return to her fiancé and her old life.

33. Your heroine is on an ancient dig when she's suddenly transported to Pompeii. She quickly realizes that Mount Vesuvius is getting ready to blow. Can she save the citizens and the man she's connected with, before the historical tragedy?

34. Your heroine is a descendant of Annie Oakley and it seems her long dead relative wants to get back into the world of the living. What happens? Does she somehow possess or coax your heroine into meeting up with Buffalo Bill's ancestor to relive old times?

35. Your heroine marries a man who only wants her so he can secure his estate. He assumes, incorrectly, that she will be easily set aside. What happens?

36. What do you do when your brother or sister is marrying the person you love? That's the case for your hero/heroine. Start your story with the brotherly/sisterly talk just before the wedding.

37. Your heroine is touring an ancient castle. She knows she has been there before. She touches something and blacks out. When she wakes, she's back in time inside the same castle. Who is she and what year is it?

38. Your heroine is on a trip and something happens that allows her to go back in time. What happens and where does she go? Does she meet anyone special? What happens when she's there?

39. Your heroine works in a candy shop. Every day she gets up early and makes delicious chocolate candies (hungry yet?). Every day the same man comes into her shop and buys a small gift box of chocolates. Who is he? Why does he buy a gift box of chocolates every day?

40. Your heroine is storming a castle with a small army. She's captured and it's discovered that she's female. What happens? Why is she storming the castle? What does the castle owner do with her?

41. Your heroine has her sights set on a nobleman. Their match would save her family. However, she yearns for him for other reasons.

Once, when she was a young girl she saw him do something that stuck with her forever. What did she see? The nobleman isn't so interested in your heroine until she captures his attention. What does she do?

42. Your heroine is caught stealing from your hero. Instead of turning her over to the authorities he decides to deal with her himself. What does he do? Why was she stealing?

43. Your heroine has just awakened to find that her garments have been removed. She's still wearing her undergarments. She asks her travel partner why he removed some, but not all, of her clothing. What does he say?

44. Your heroine is touring an old vineyard. She breaks away from the group and finds herself deep in the old wine cellars. She pulls a bottle of wine out of the racks and suddenly finds herself... Where does she travel in time and who is waiting there for her?

45. Your hero has agreed to wed a monster in order to save his family and his younger sisters. Yet on the day of his wedding someone else catches his eye. What happens?

46. Your heroine has no desire to ever get married, yet she does agree to pose as someone's wife. Why? What happens?

47. Your heroine is being coveted by a frightening and powerful man. To escape his advances she puts her attention onto someone else. Who and what happens?

48. Your heroine has married a few times and each time her husband dies before they can consummate their marriage. What does she do when she meets the man of her dreams?

49. Your hero has fallen for the new schoolteacher in town. Before he can say hello his enemy has swept her off her feet. How does he get her attention and save her from making a huge mistake?

50. Your heroine uncovers saucy love letters from the past. She becomes obsessed with them and the people who wrote them. She starts digging and finds…What does she find?

51. Your heroine's sister is betrothed to a man. Rather than face him, she's run away. Your heroine steps in to take her sister's place, until someone can find her sister. When her sister comes home, your heroine's not so sure she wants to step aside. What happens?

52. Your hero is on a trek to meet with another family and forge a union between them by whatever means necessary. If he fails, all is lost. When he arrives on the edge of the family's territory he is met with a huge surprise. What happens?

53. He has one goal, to ruin your heroine's reputation and thus discredit her family. Will your hero go through with it? How does he try to ruin her reputation and what happens?

54. Your heroine is on her own. Her husband is dead, her estate is gone and she has to start over. She heads to the city and discovers…What happens? What does she learn about herself?

55. Your heroine has a secret; she poses for nude paintings and sculptures. What happens when her secret is uncovered?

56. Your hero is escorting your heroine to her future husband. Trouble is, he wants her for himself. What happens?

57. Your heroine is a tapestry expert. She is in an old castle evaluating a tapestry. She pulls back the fabric hanging on a wall and is transported back in time. Now she's the one making the tapestry for a wealthy nobleman. What happens?

58. Your heroine blames your hero for the death of her husband. She vows revenge. What happens?

59. Your heroine was born in the wrong century. She loves tinkering with cars. She loves sports and she enjoys working with her hands. She's given up hope finding a man who understands her until your hero walks through the door. Who is he and what happens?

60. Your heroine has suffered the greatest tragedy. Her husband and daughter died. She buys a house in a remote location to hide and live her life alone. Only the caretaker won't let her. He seems intent on making sure she's okay. Who is he? Why does he care? What happens?

61. It's the middle of the Civil War and your hero has fallen for someone he shouldn't. Who has he fallen for and what happens?

62. It's the gold rush in Alaska and your heroine owns a bar and hotel. What does she do when the man who broke her heart years ago walks back through her doors?

63. Your heroine is asked to chaperone her cousin for the summer. Her cousin is a bit of a handful, but it's her cousin's fiancé that causes her the most trouble. Why? What happens?

64. When burns scarred your heroine as a young child she realized that she would never marry. Your hero fights hard to get past your heroine's tough exterior to show her that she's worthy of love, passion, and marriage.

65. Your hero and heroine are married. The trouble is, their spouses are cheating on them with each other. When their cheating spouses die, the town's gossips begin whispering. What do your hero and heroine do to move past the betrayal and the town's gossip?

66. Your heroine is on the Titanic. What happens when she sees her first love on board the fated ship?

67. Your heroine possesses a device that allows her to travel back and forth to one single place in time. She has essentially been living two lives. What happens when she becomes stuck in the past? Where in time does she travel to?

68. Your hero's wife disappeared almost ten years ago. What does he do when she reappears and says she's been to the future?

69. Your hero and heroine are on an airplane. As it flies through the infamous Bermuda triangle it disappears. Where do they go? What happens?

70. Your heroine is out on a date with a scientist. He is smitten with her and decides to pull both of them back in time together. However, he doesn't count on her being

spitting mad at him nor does he expect her to fall for someone from the past.

71. Your heroine is a writer. She's just taken a night security job at an art museum so she can write while she works. She finds a nude statue to be an inspiration for a character in her book. She doesn't expect the statue to come alive. Who is he?

72. Your heroine receives a letter on her 25th birthday. It's dated 100 years ago to the day and it predicts her future. What does it say?

73. Your heroine is sailing when she discovers what seems to be an abandoned boat. She boards it only to find a man from the past. What happens?

74. One wrong choice sends your hero back in time to fix the past mistakes of his great grandfather. What happens? Who does he meet? How does he change the past and subsequently change his own future?

75. Your heroine is on a date with a man she's had a crush on for months. They're riding their bikes in the countryside when suddenly they're no longer in this time period and they're no longer on bikes – they're on horses. They arrive in the middle of a battle and are mistaken for..? What happens?

76. Your hero spent most of his childhood and teenage years on an aircraft carrier that was turned into a museum. He is certain the place is haunted.

What he's not prepared for is the night he encounters a woman on the ship. She's not sure how she got there or what year it is. Who is she? Why is she on the boat?

77. Your heroine was in a car accident. The injury resulted in her memory being completely erased. Yet whenever she plays the piano in her home she's transported back in time. Piece by piece she's able to put her life, and her memory, back together. Along the way she finds new love. What happens?

78. Someone pushes your heroine over the edge of a cliff. As she falls, certain she's heading to her death, she blacks out. Where does she wake up and what year is it?

79. Your hero is intrigued by a black cat that has been following him all day. It seems the cat wants his attention. He follows it. What does he see?

80. Your heroine is on a vacation with her new boyfriend. She's having a terrible time. All he wants to do is lounge around the hotel. She wants to get out and sightsee. She gets out on her own, falls down a well and…what happens?

81. Your heroine is entering her strawberry shortcake into the annual country fair baking contest. She sets her cake down on the judging table and suddenly it's 1950. What happens?

82. Your heroine just started working at a new restaurant. She opens the refrigerator and food tumbles out at her feet. The refrigerator is a mess. She turns around to ask for help and realizes she's not in the restaurant kitchen anymore.

Behind her is a famous, and long dead, chef and they're asking her to quickly bring the eggs. What happens? Where is she and who is the famous chef?

83. All your heroine has ever longed for is a slow and romantic courtship. The men she's dated have all been the

exact opposite. They don't have a romantic bone in their body – they just want sex and ...well, sex. That is until she meets your hero. But then again, he's not from this time period. Who is he?

84. Your heroine is laid up in the hospital having just had surgery. Her sister in law brings her more than a few dozen romantic novels. Your heroine, having nothing else to do, begins reading. She also begins seeing things like the hero in the regency novel walking past her door. What happens?

85. Your heroine is at a baseball game. She gets hit in the head by a fly ball. When she wakes up, she doesn't know who anyone is and she's certain that she's traveled in time. What year is it? What happens?

86. On a mountain hike your hero doesn't see the approaching storm until it is too late. He's struck by lightning and zapped into another time. What happens?

87. Your heroine breeds champion horses, and someone is trying to sabotage her. She hires a handsome detective to figure it out. What happens?

88. Your hero is a detective hired by a socialite to find out if her son's betrothed is a virgin. What happens?

89. Your heroine knows she has had past lives. In fact, she dreams about one particular past life repeatedly. She meets a man and knows him instantly. Who is he and what happens?

90. Your heroine hates it when people talk down to her. Yet that's exactly what her soon to be husband does. He's patronizing, condescending, and a genuine bore – when he's not treating her like a child, he's ignoring her. What

does she do to prove to him that she's not only intelligent; she's smarter than he is?

91. You heroine lives in the 1960s. She's doing what she's supposed to do – working in the steno pool and waiting for a proposal so she can pop out the 2.5 kids and live happily ever after.

She's running an errand for someone else, she takes a wrong turn and ends up in a dark alley. Someone is behind her. She's terrified. Fumbling in the dark, she's searching for a weapon to defend herself when she finds a door knob. She turns the knob and ends up in 2012. What happens?

92. Your heroine is a Victorian horticulturist. She loves plants. On an expedition to the jungle to study native plants she meets her very own Tarzan. How does she meet him?

93. Your heroine is out for a morning hike with her dog. She comes across a rock formation that intrigues her. She touches it and suddenly she's back in time – Paleolithic times, but she's not alone.

There are others who have been zapped back in time. They're all from different periods. She meets one person that she connects with. Who does she meet and what happens?

94. Your heroine has snuck into a masquerade ball. Her objective is to humiliate someone. Why? What happens?

95. Your heroine has the ability to astral travel back and forth in time. She has a favorite time period that she returns to again and again. Why?

96. It's the first Kentucky Derby and your heroine is in the stands with her fists clenched. Why?

97. It's the 1853 World's Fair and your heroine is standing atop the Latting Observatory. Why is she there? Describe what she sees.

98. Your heroine finds comfort in the gardens of a nearby estate. She falls asleep in the main greenhouse and is awakened by something surprising. What happens?

99. Your heroine's father has been captured and no one seems to be willing to do anything about it. She convinces the leader of a small band of men to help her rescue her father. What happens?

100. Your heroine has a wild side, wilder than most men her age. When a pirate ship docks nearby she cannot resist tempting the handsome captain. What happens?

Notes:

_____
_____
_____
_____
_____
_____
_____
_____
_____
_____
_____
_____
_____
_____

Chapter 2

Contemporary Romance, Romantic Comedy, Mainstream

101. Your hero is using the men's room in a large hotel. He is washing his hands when a woman comes out of one of the bathroom stalls. She holds her finger to her lips. She wants him to stay silent. Who is she? Why is she in the men's bathroom?

102. A woman on the run finds $500,000. She knows who it belongs to; a sexy stranger who helped her out of a dangerous situation. What does she do with the money?

103. Tacky Terri, it's what they called her in junior high, in high school, in college and probably what they call her behind her back at the accounting firm where she works.

It's time to let go of her nerdy look, the look everyone else in her family has had since the early 1950's. Spending her hard earned savings on a complete overhaul in New York, she's ready for a new life, and a new man.

But is she ready for the attention she gets? What happens, who does she meet and how does she handle it?

104. Your mild mannered heroine is having a horrible day.

Her car won't start. This forces her to walk home from work where she's just been laid off. On her walk home she comes across a man who is harassing a woman.

Fed up with the way people treat each other, she steps in to help and ends up in the hospital.

105. A female sportscaster, tired of being hit on by athletes, finally meets the man of her dreams. Who is he and how do they meet?

Remember conflict makes for a great story!

106. A life change motivates your heroine to start connecting with old friends and classmates on a social networking website.

When she finds her high school crush online she's both delighted and dismayed – he's still single and assuming his online photo is accurate he's also very very hot.

When she finds out he's living in her city (not her home town, but someplace she's moved to) she cannot resist tracking him down.

What does she do? What happens next?

How is he different than she remembers?

107. Your heroine is heading to her mother's to celebrate Mother's Day. Her Mother has remarried. Your heroine is surprised to learn her new stepfather has a son who is her age. When he walks in the door she.....

What happens next? For example, is he someone she had a one night stand with? Is he someone she got into a car accident with? Her therapist? Or is he simply a beautiful man who makes her heart beat double time?

108. Your heroine wakes up with a very sexy man in bed with her. He's passed out. She can't wake him. On her finger is a wedding ring. What happened? Are they married? Who is the guy in her bed?

109. Your heroine is having a milestone birthday and decides to do something crazy. What does she do? Who does she meet along the way and how does her milestone birthday affect their interaction?

110. Your heroine is a no holds barred, powerful, negotiator. She's often brought in to being unions and other parties to their knees.

When she's hired by one of the country's largest companies to conduct hard ball negotiations with the owner of a smaller company, she's stunned to find that she's not only met her match, she also – for the first time in her life – isn't sure she wants to win this one.

111. Your heroine is taking the trip of a lifetime. Heart filled with excitement she boards the plane. As she makes her way down the aisle to her seat she sees him. Where is she going and why? Who does she see and how does it affect her?

112. Your heroine is cycling through the city, perhaps on a country road or in the mountains (you decide) when she is in a bike accident. She hits her head (yes, she is wearing a helmet) and blacks out.

When she wakes up she doesn't know where she is. Worse, she doesn't know the man taking care of her. Who is he? What happens?

113. Your heroine feels like she's used up her "Risk taking" quota for the year. She left her hometown of 25 years to take a new job half way across the country.

She doesn't know anyone and is on her own and away from her family for the first time ever. At a Labor Day party with her new co-workers things get a little silly. Someone double dares her to do something crazy. After enough goading and a little imbibing she takes her up on the dare and runs smack dab into... him.

Who is he? What is his reaction to her daring behavior? What was she dared to do?

114. It's a beautiful sunny day at the pumpkin patch. Your heroine is working and loving her life. She sees a small child take a tumble from a hay ride cart. A horse from a cart following behind is headed straight for the child. Your heroine dives in and saves the kid.

The father is grateful and asks your heroine out for dinner to repay her. He's a single dad and attractive. What does your heroine do? Does she go out with him? Why or why not?

115. Your hero and heroine are both running in the famous New York City Marathon. They don't know each other, but they meet and support each other along the way. They finish the race together and part awkwardly – surrounded by celebrating friends and family they don't even get to say goodbye.

They meet unexpectedly again sometime later. Write that scene. Where do they meet? What happens?

116. In honor of Les Miserables, Like Crazy, and a few other stories, your hero and heroine meet. Perhaps they're on vacation, perhaps one of them is dying – you decide. Regardless, they only have this one day together. What do they do?

117. This story starter begins at midnight on New Year's Eve. Your heroine is determined to start this year off right. When the clock strikes 12 on New Year's Eve she grabs the closest man next to her and plants a big one on him.

What happens next?

118. Your heroine is doing something that makes her feel like a kid again. Maybe she's roller skating. Maybe she's surfing or building a sand castle. Maybe she's climbing a tree, fixing a car, or playing kickball.

As she's in her bliss and enjoying her childhood passion, she's being watched by someone. Who is he? Why is he watching her? How do they meet?

119. Your heroine is getting her fortune told. Maybe she's doing it on a whim or maybe she believes in the paranormal (you decide). The fortune teller tells her something shocking about her future. What does she learn and what does she do with the information?

120. Your heroine, a rock climbing instructor, lost her first love in a climbing accident and refuses to date adrenaline junkies. When she falls for a photographer, she feels she's finally found someone 'safe.', when something tragic happens, she realizes that life's too short. What happens?

121. As a temporary executive assistant, your heroine has the skills to step into a high powered office and make her mark. Being a temp also offers her the freedom and flexibility to work where and when she wants to.

When an unexpected event forces her to take a job at the last place on earth she wants to work, she is forced to make nice with a man she detests. What happens to cause her to have to take the job and what happens when she gets there?

122. Your heroine was a stockbroker with one of the most successful companies in the country. When the company goes belly up, she decides to make lemons from lemonade and pursue her dream life. Where does she go and what does she do?

123. Your heroine is living her ideal life in sunny California, well ideal except for the fact that she's still single. When a family tragedy strikes, and she's pulled back to her dreary old home town, she learns there's more to her home town than she remembers – including a sexy man.

Why does she get pulled home? What keeps her there for an extended period of time? Who does she meet or reconnect with? Does she stay in her home town or go back to sunny California?

124. An injured race car driver falls for his doctor (who nurses him back to health). What is the internal and external conflict for both characters?

125. Two days before her wedding, a journalist sees a photo of a man while researching a story. She's compelled to find him. Why? What happens? Who is he?

126. On vacation with her friend everything goes wrong for your heroine. Her friends hook up with strangers, she nearly drowns and she gets the sunburn of the century.

To top it all off gets food poisoning and someone steals her traveler's checks. It turns out to be the best vacation she ever has. Why? What happens to turn it around?

127. Your heroine just inherited millions and suddenly every Tom, Dick and Harry she's ever dated is calling and trying to rekindle their old flame.

When a particular old flame calls her heart really does skip a beat. Can she trust that his feelings are real, or is he just like all the others and only after her money?

128. A youth soccer coach is used to getting yelled at by overeager and overprotective helicopter parents. One single dad really pushes her, buttons. When she's accidentally locked in a storage shed with him all heck breaks out. What happens?

129. A publicity specialist has a new job. To overhaul the city's most notorious man and give him a new image. It's a tough enough job as it is, and it's made even more difficult by the fact that she has the hots for him. Why does he need his image overhauled? What does she do to help him?

130. Your heroine, a professional poker player, is on a losing streak, both in men and in cards. Until she meets a new man. Is he her new good luck charm? Who is he? What does he do? How does he turn your heroine's luck around?

131. Your heroine is a kid at heart. On her way to work she is sidetracked by a toy store. She goes inside and meets a man. What happens?

132. Your heroine is getting a lecture from a well-intentioned, but not so supportive mother on the sidewalk in a big city. A man, overhearing the lecture, steps behind the mom and starts mimicking her. Does your heroine laugh? Does she get ticked off and yell at the man? What

happens? Who is this man and how do he and your heroine get together?

133. Your heroine has agreed to be a surrogate mother for her cousin/sister/friend. However, being pregnant isn't what she thought it'd be - especially when she has the hots for her new doctor. What happens when the baby comes?

134. Your heroine is house sitting and caring for her neighbor's dog while the man/woman is out of town. While trying to retrieve the cat who has lodged himself under the bed she finds a shoebox of letters from an old flame. What does she do with the letters? What happens?

135. Your heroine is a race car driver. When a new owner buys the team she must find a way to get past his chauvinistic ways to keep her dream job.

She's a smart ass and a mischievous woman. How does she convince him that women are capable of more than cooking and screwing – they can be darned good drivers too?

136. Your heroine has synesthesia. What senses does she combine and what does she experience? Open your story with her perceptions.

137. Your heroine has been waiting in a bar for a girlfriend to arrive. Her girlfriend is late. She starts people watching and notices a single dad out with his daughter.

The daughter has a temper tantrum. Your heroine…laughs, buys him a beer, or perhaps distracts the girl with something shiny from her purse. You decide what happens next.

138. Your heroine is an up and coming professional golfer. When a lifelong golfing idol and role model sexually harasses her she gets the upper hand. What does she do and what sexy man witnesses the entire encounter?

139. Your heroine enters her craft beer in the local festival and wins first prize. In addition to ticking off the Barley Brothers – who have won for the past four years and were counting on five in a row – she's captured the attention of another. Who is he and what does he want?

140. Your heroine is zipping down the highway when she gets pulled over. Turns out the car she's driving is stolen. What happens next?

141. Your heroine walks into a pet store where the owner is naming the animals. She decides to help him. Why is he naming them?

142. Your hero gets a 'butt dial' and your heroine is unaware her entire conversation is being heard by a total stranger. What is she talking about and what does he do when the phone finally disconnects?

143. Your heroine has set her New Year's Resolution. She is giving herself one year to find a husband. It's now Dec 30th and she has one more day left to find the man of her dreams. Where does she find him?

144. Your heroine is camping with her girlfriends. She has had too much to drink and passes out in her tent. In the middle of the night she gets up to go to the bathroom. Stumbling back she climbs into the wrong tent at the wrong campsite. Who does she wake up next to?

145. Your heroine is out for a walk when she sees a dog struggling on an icy pond. She rushes out to help him and ends up needing a bit of help herself. A man runs to her rescue and the two of them bring the dog to safety. What happens next?

146. Your hero is out playing darts at the local bar. Distracted by one sexy, scantily clad woman, he throws his dart and hits another. What happens next?

147. Your hero/heroine is at a rock concert with friends. The friends accidentally leave without him/her. What happens next?

148. Your heroine is teaching a man how to blow smoke rings. Why?

149. It's Halloween and your heroine is at a party. What costume is she wearing? What costume is your hero wearing? How do they meet?

150. Your heroine is at a wedding. She's drunk. What does your hero do to save her before she does something embarrassing?

151. Your hero is lost. He stops to ask for directions, much to the surprise of the woman he asks. What happens next?

152. Your heroine just discovered that her boss may be illegally wiretapping local politicians to get the inside scoop for his newspaper. Trouble is, she has a huge crush on him. What does she do?

153. Your heroine gets a new pair of glasses, but someone has mixed her prescription up with another patient's. Who is he and can she see what he looks like without her glasses?

154. Your heroine is looking for love online – rather she's Googling old boyfriends to find out what they're up to. She starts communicating with her "first" and they set up a time to meet. When she gets there she learns that she's been communicating with the wrong guy! What happens next?

155. Your heroine owns a company that holds and organizes endurance sporting events, such as adventure races, 100 mile races and cross country races. When an entire team disappears she takes it on herself to find them. She's joined by the brother of one of the missing teammates. What happens?

156. Your heroine has two personalities (or more). Her crazier personality is looking for: Elvis, Jesus, Shakespeare, and Davy Jones – you choose who she's looking for. The normal personality keeps waking up in strange situations. Start your story with your heroine's normal personality waking up.

157. What would you do if you couldn't fail? What would your protagonist do? What trouble does it get her into?

158. Your heroine is about to walk across hot coals – literally. Why is she doing it?

159. Your protagonist is a high school sports coach who has a crush on their star player's single parent. How does the coach manipulate a way to meet the parent and what happens?

160. Your heroine lives by Lana Turner's philosophy, "A successful man is one who makes more money than his wife can spend. A successful woman is one who can find such a man." How does she learn this isn't the way to her happiness?

161. Your heroine's car needs repair, again. She takes it back to the hunky mechanic who is starting to believe that she's either a horrible driver or she's breaking her car intentionally. Start your story with his reaction to her bringing her car in again.

162. Your heroine's idea of a dream date is the opera. Her date takes her to a monster truck rally. What happens when she tries to sneak out?

163. She remembered the feeling of seeing the spinning bottle eventually point to him. Now fifteen years later he still made her feel….

164. It's Valentine's Day and your heroine hates the holiday. She lives fully by the quote, "People call it Valentine's Day. I call it singles awareness day." What does she see and experience that changes her mind?

165. Your heroine has started a new job. She cannot resist snooping in her boss's desk while he's away. She didn't intend to snoop, but is tempted when she's in his office. She opens a drawer and finds something unexpected. What does she find?

166. Your hero accidentally picks up the wrong cell phone. He calls his phone to try to find it, and hears a sexy voice on the other end of the line. Who is she and how did she get his phone?

167. Your heroine is a blogger who reviews books. She blasts a popular horror novelist and is surprised when he shows up on her front porch. What happens next?

168. Your heroine is a bodyguard. It's a male dominated industry. How does she handle the chauvinistic attitude of her new rock star client?

169. Your heroine is a writer/blogger/journalist. She's working from her apartment or condo when she looks out her window and sees a moose in the pool.

It can't get out of the pool and is struggling. She rushes out to help and is joined by a man who also lives in the condo complex. What happens next?

170. Your heroine is out for a walk or a jog and overhears a juicy conversation. What do they hear and how do they react?

171. Your heroine is learning to drive. Her driving instructor is so attractive he's making her nervous and she keeps making mistakes. How does she resolve the problem?

172. Your protagonist is a pediatrician. A caregiver (maybe a single parent or an aunt) brings a young child into the office with ear pain. What does your hero/heroine find inside the child's ear and what happens next? You could do this with a veterinarian and a pet too.

173. Your heroine is a health and wellness coach with a dark and unhealthy secret. What is it? How does admitting it or trying to change the habit, change her life?

174. Your heroine just started a new receptionist job. She's talking to a friend on the phone about the hot guy she works with. She doesn't realize that the intercom is on and everyone, including the hot guy, can hear her conversation. What happens next?

175. Your heroine is in the hospital. She hears voices. She cannot open her eyes or speak. What does she hear?

176. Everything is going right for your heroine. She's a dress designer and an Oscar nominee is wearing her design to the awards show. Her boyfriend was just promoted at the law firm and she just won a Caribbean vacation on a radio call in show. With everything going so right, why is she so unhappy?

177. Your hero falls for the raspy voice of a woman on the radio. He begins dreaming about her and hearing her voice everywhere. He tracks her down. What happens?

178. Your heroine is an MMA (Mixed Martial Arts) fighter. It's a tough life and it makes it difficult to find a man. She finally meets a man she feels a connection with. Yet she is afraid to tell him what she does for a living. How does she break the news and how does he react?

179. Your heroine just opened a bakery and has the opportunity to compete in a cupcake contest. Trouble is, the jerk across town is competing too. The winner receives national recognition for their bakery and $50,000. Who wins the competition and how do these two competitors fall in love?

180. Your hero is taking a nap on his back porch when a not so graceful burglar trips over him. He's intrigued by her cat suit and her ill-fated career choice, but obviously the fact that she was going to rob him hasn't passed his attention. What happens next?

181. Your heroine is looking up old boyfriends online one night when she discovers her first love has placed a "Wife Wanted" advertisement in the local paper. She applies for

the job. What happens and why does he need to advertise for a wife?

182. Your heroine starts a roller derby club and has to talk the best coach into joining her team. How does she do it?

183. Your heroine's mother is homeless. Despite all of your heroine's efforts her mother's mental instability keeps her on the street. Now she's dead and your heroine will stop at nothing to find out who killed her.

184. Your heroine owns a failing cupcake shop. No one in her small town appreciates her fine baking nor the cuteness and practicality of a good cupcake.

She decides to add an attraction to her cupcake shop that's sure to draw in the crowds. It's a last ditch attempt to save her shop. What does she do? What is the town's reaction?

185. Your hero has just returned to from the war. Everyone hails him a hero, but the last thing he wants to do is talk about his wartime adventures. He just wants to forget. He rents a cabin in the woods to get away from it all.

However, his cabin has a neighbor and she's turning into a better distraction that he could possibly imagine, until she gets too close. Why is she at the cabin and what happens between them?

186. Your heroine's first day working as the marketing exec for a ski resort and she's in a car accident. Driving in snow is new to her. Heck, everything about snow is new to her. Who does she run into? What happens?

187. Your heroine is a restaurant critic and she's just had the worst pizza of her life. The restaurant's owner comes

out to give her a piece of his mind and all she wants is a piece of something else. Their interaction is heated. What happens?

188. Your heroine has never driven a car in her life. Her friend, and ride home, has broken the designated driver rule and she's drunk. Now your heroine has to figure out how to get them both homes safely.

They're not in the city (so a cab isn't an option) and they don't know anyone in the bar – asking for a ride home from a stranger isn't a good idea. So she drives. And of course she's pulled over by the local police. She tries to flirt her way out of a ticket. He's not buying it. What happens?

189. Your heroine has fallen for a man who comes into her coffee shop/restaurant/store every week. Unfortunately, he doesn't speak English. She takes Spanish classes to learn how to communicate with him. What's the first thing she says to him?

190. A woman is on a long trip on her motorcycle. She's covering the country from one end to the other. Maybe she's just ended a painful marriage or maybe she's writing a book about the trip.

You decide.

She ends up at a biker bar to grab some lunch and a group of men hassle her. It's nothing she hasn't handled before only this time they're not taking 'no' for an answer and she's beginning to get worried.

Oh, she has a gun and she's not afraid to use it. Still, things could go wrong. Another biker senses her anxiety and steps in to help. Who is he and what does he do to help?

191. Your heroine works at a coffee shop. She overhears a conversation about something complicated like nuclear physics. She mutters something under her breath when they get some data wrong. One of the 'brainiacs' hears her. The attractive one. He approaches her. What does he say?

192. Your heroine is a teacher. She befriends a young student who is gay and dealing with some personal issues. She lets him stay at her place and that's when the problems start. What happens?

193. Your heroine is a writer. She spends 90% of her time in her apartment. Human connection is found on televisions and social networking. Her therapist tells her to get out of the house and connect with people. She joins a dodge ball team. What happens?

194. Your heroine or hero walks downstairs to find a strange dog inside their home. Where'd the dog come from?

195. Your heroine heads out on what she hopes will be a life changing 'Eat, Pray, Love' kind of year. Instead of learning and finding herself, everything goes wrong. What happens?

196. Your hero is a ski instructor who has a firm rule; no dating the clients. He has learned the hard way too many times. Yet there's something about this new client that may make him break his rule. What is it? What makes her special?

197. Your heroine forgot about daylight savings time and is late for the most important meeting of her life. What happens?

198. Your hero's dad has just married a younger woman; much younger. He reluctantly visits his dad and discovers his new step mom has a sister. How do you ask your aunt out on a date?

199. Your hero and heroine meet at summer camp when they're younger. It's love at first sight, however as summer camps go, they never see each other again – until now. How do the reunite?

200. Your heroine owns a flower shop and her favorite client keeps trying to set her up with her son. The man is a dowdy dud, so she politely refuses. But when a rival sets up shop across town, your heroine needs to keep her biggest client happy. What happens?

201. Your heroine is vacationing in Greece when she is arrested for protesting. She was just trying to get through the crowd. In jail she meets a handsome Greek man with a passion for his cause. What happens?

202. An elephant trainer at the circus falls for an animal rights activist. How do they meet?

203. A gust of wind blows your heroine down onto her backside. Does your hero laugh or catch her as she's falling?

204. Your hero or heroine gets a stalker; a kitty. The cat keeps following them wherever they go. Why?

205. Someone gives your hero or heroine a pet monkey. Why? What do they do with it?

206. Your hero or heroine's new neighbors are throwing a party, a loud one. Finally at 3 am they've had enough.

He/she walks over to the neighbors to complain. What happens?

207. Your heroine is the assistant to one of the premier party planners in the country. On the day of one of their biggest parties of the year, her boss disappears. Now it's your heroine's job to pull off the party on her own and that means dealing directly with the client, a man she's had a crush on for years.

208. Your heroine is in the Deep South. She's from Minnesota. She's lost. She's stopped at a gas station to get directions, but neither she nor the gas station attendant understands what the other person is saying. A handsome man steps in to serve as translator. What happens next?

209. Your hero is making a movie. He has the top producers behind him; all he needs to do is convince an A-list actress that she's perfect for the part. What does he do to convince her?

210. Your heroine is jogging through the park. She twists her ankle right in front of a good looking guy sitting on a park bench. He thinks she is faking to get his attention. What happens next?

211. Your heroine is going down her first ski run of the day. She wipes out and blows out her knee. She's rescued by a handsome ski patrolman. What happens next?

212. Your heroine is taking a road trip to find a new life. She's literally taking turns and stopping in towns as she is inspired to do so. On the road for a few months now she's had only positive experiences.

Only now she's wound up in a town that is unwelcoming and she's stuck there. Why is she stuck? Why are they unwelcoming? What does she do?

213. Your heroine is lounging on the deck of a yacht. The sun beats down on her. A cool breeze helps her stay comfortable. Beautiful music is playing in the background and she has a bowl of delicious fruit by her side. All is right with the world. What happens to blow it all away?

214. Your heroine is pounding the pavement looking for a job. She's just had a door slammed in her face, literally. What does she do?

215. Your hero's girlfriend just won the lottery. How does he react?

216. Your hero, or heroine, is filling in, temporarily, for the family business. Start your story with their first day.

217. Your heroine is a personal trainer and her boyfriend is a couch potato. He's feeling insecure and does something crazy. What does he do and how does she react?

218. Your heroine was shot in the head when she was a child. It was a domestic violence incident. How did that event change her life? Did it give her some sort of 6th sense?

Did it cause her to live on the street? Did she make it her life's crusade to protect children? You decide how that event changed your heroine and made her who she is. Then, start your story there. Put her in the middle of a situation that reflects who she is and what she's about.

219. Your hero is in the midst of a panic attack. Why? What is causing it?

220. Your heroine is ticking something off of her bucket list. What is it?

221. Your heroine is a camp counselor and things are going wrong at her camp. She turns to the boy's camp across the lake for help. What's going on at her camp?

222. Your hero and heroine are walking down the street. They're both listening to music and not paying attention. They bump into each other, apologize, take the earbuds out and realize they're listening to the same song. What happens next?

223. Your hero just learned that his dad isn't really his dad. What does he do next?

224. Your heroine is leaving a coffee shop when a rude man pushes past her causing her to spill coffee all over herself. Another man is watching. What does he do?

225. Your heroine is late for work. She's running through the parking lot/structure and runs into her very attractive boss. What does she say? What's her excuse?

226. Your heroine hit "Reply all" on a sensitive email meant for only one person. What does the email say? What happens?

227. Your heroine accidentally dials her mom's cell phone number. She thinks she's calling her boyfriend. What happens?

228. Your heroine is in the men's bathroom (you decide why) and she sees or hears something she's not supposed

to. What does she see or hear and what does she do about it?

229. Your hero starts the story with the worst pick up line ever. What does he say and how does the woman (maybe your heroine, maybe not) react?

230. Your heroine or hero is taking a trip (you decide if it is business or pleasure). They're upgraded to first class and wind up sitting next to….

231. Your heroine's ex-boyfriend published a sex video and now everyone wants to know if she's the woman in the video. Is she? You decide. The video has brought her a significant amount of attention; some wanted, some unwanted. Start your story where she's receiving some attention for the video.

232. A blackmailer destroyed her family and your heroine is out for revenge. First she'll start with the blackmailer's son. How does she plan on getting revenge?

233. Your heroine is getting ready to launch a new shoe line. Everything she has is sunk into this business venture. It's the big night, the night of her fashion show, and something goes dreadfully wrong. What? Is she able to recover? Who helps her?

234. Your heroine is a caddy for a female golf pro. It's her dream job. What does your heroine do when the golf pro's coach, and boyfriend, hits on her?

235. Your hero/heroine has narcolepsy. They've just fallen asleep. Where? What happens?

236. Your hero is jogging on a narrow trail deep in the woods. Your heroine is jogging too. She's coming from the other direction. The woods are peaceful. The sky is blue and the birds are singing. One of them has a dog. What happens when their paths cross?

237. Your heroine works at an auto body shop. The police raid the shop on a tip that they're stripping stolen cars. Your heroine argues with one of the officers/detectives. Describe the interaction.

238. The roads are treacherous. Icy and dangerous. No one should be on them, but your heroine has to get to her patient's house – she's getting ready to deliver a baby. Your heroine is in an accident.

She spins out and smashes her car against a tree. A car stops to help. She asks the driver to take her to her patient's house. What happens next?

239. Your heroine finds her boss cheating on his wife. She accidentally spills the beans to a friend and it eventually gets back to her boss's wife. Now she's out of a job. She cannot afford her rent and her boyfriend broke up with her. Now what?

240. Your heroine runs a multinational corporation. Unfortunately, she can't handle basic tasks like cooking and cleaning. After losing her business in a takeover, she's back to bare bones and decides to embrace it by taking a cooking class. Who does she meet in the class?

241. Your heroine comes home exhausted after a long and difficult day. All she wants is to put her feet up, eat a nice dinner, and relax. She sits down on the couch, puts her feet up, and ....what happens?

242. Your hero is a police officer who is beginning to suspect that his new partner has multiple personalities. What is she doing that makes him believe this and what does he do about it?

243. Your hero is the most hated man in the world; he's an IRS investigator. What does he do when he falls for the woman he's investigating?

244. Your hero is a pickpocket hired by a woman to steal…? What does she hire him to steal and why?

245. Your hero is smitten with an outdoorsy girl and has been faking his abilities and interest in all things outdoors. She plans a surprise mountain biking or rock climbing date, he doesn't know how to mountain bike or rock climb. What happens?

246. Your heroine's mom has just been released from a mental hospital and is in her care. Start your story when your heroine is going out on a first date and her mom is causing problems.

247. Your heroine catches her boyfriend kissing her sister. What happens next?

248. Your heroine, a police officer, falls for the owner of a medical marijuana dispensary. How do they meet?

249. Your heroine is dumped by her boyfriend. She hooks up with her roommate's best friend on the rebound. What happens?

250. Your heroine's son's dog is hit by a car. A witness rushes to the dog's aid, helps them get to the emergency

veterinarian and helps put a smile on her son's face. What happens next?

Notes:

_____

_____

_____

_____

_____

_____

_____

_____

_____

_____

_____

_____

_____

_____

_____

_____

_____

_____

_____

_____

_____

_____

_____

_____

_____

Chapter 3

Fantasy, Urban Fantasy, Paranormal Romance, Steampunk

251. Your heroine is on a ghost tour with friends. She is a skeptic, but the leader of the tour is hot, so she keeps her sarcastic comments to herself – mostly. When something grabs her by the arm she turns to find that there's no one behind or beside her. What happens next?

252. Your heroine has become the carrier for an otherworldly creature. She's the host for it and must turn to experimental scientists to help her separate from this entity. In the lab she meets someone. Who does she meet and why is he in the lab?

253. Your hero awakes from an extremely vivid dream. A mysterious woman is in the dream. At the end of the dream he dies. Your hero awakes just as he's dying in his dream and feels he must find the woman. If not, the dream will surely come true. Who is the woman? What happens?

254. Your heroine can tell when people are going to die. It's a curse. She sees it as clear as day. Unfortunately, she can only see it when their death is imminent.

She meets a man, they hit it off extremely well and she thinks she may have finally met "the one," when she sees his death. He's going to be killed.

What does she do? Does she tell him about her ability? Does she try to stop the death? Does she try to sacrifice herself to save him?

255. A woman has a secret. She has wings and can fly. For this reason she cannot get close to anyone and love is not an option. She trusted once and almost lost her life.

Now when her life is on the line again (you decide why) one man may be the secret to her survival. Who is he and why will he save her?

256. Your heroine and your hero are digging a well. Actually, your hero is digging it for your heroine. She's paying him for the work and overseeing the project. They discover a small machine buried in a box about six feet down. What does the machine do? What do they do when they discover it?

257. A woman, your heroine, owns a small town beauty shop. It does well and she makes a good living, and she keeps tabs on all the town gossip. But when a mysterious woman/couple/man moves in and casts a spell to steal all of your heroine's clients, she's not going to take it.

Mustering up all her courage, she marches right up to the doorstep of the most powerful man in town. Nope, not the mayor and not the sheriff either. She goes straight to the top – to the town's mysterious and intensely handsome benefactor, and it's rumored he's a warlock.

She's gone to him for a favor. Will she be willing to pay his price? What is his price? What happens?

258. It's the last day of the world (you decide why this is the case – maybe some country is dropping a nuclear bomb or

maybe the planets are too close and they're going to collide). Your story opens up with your heroine preparing for it. (I think it would be fun to approach this dismal subject as a romantic comedy, or hey, maybe a paranormal or fantasy approach would be more appropriate.)

Of course she survives the event and the rest of the story can be about how she survives. How her life changes and who she meets along the way.

259. Your heroine is a good fairy. Her nemesis is a bad fairy. They haven't seen each other in years, and spy each other across the room. Where are they? Why are they enemies? What happens?

260. One man holds the power to control the world. (You decide what his powerful gift is.) He was born with this gift and has been imprisoned and carefully guarded all his life.

Now he's escaped and your heroine is the only person who can find him. She has seen his power first hand. She too has a powerful gift and spent some time with him, locked up, as a child.

But it's been ten years since she's seen him. She's been hunting for weeks and suddenly he's there in front of her.

What happens when they come face to face?

261. Your heroine is a scientist and a workaholic. She brings her work home with her sometimes. Living alone, it's not a problem. There's little risk.

Course she wouldn't mind bumping into her new neighbor more often. She's working on a new project late one night when she sees something hideous emerge from her neighbor's basement. What does she see? What does she do? Who or what is it that lives in her neighbor's house?

262. Your heroine is at a museum (renaissance, Wild West, civil war... you decide – choose the time period that intrigues and excites you).

She tries on a period costume and is instantly connected to the original owner. Why? Because she was the original owner – she's been reincarnated. It sparks a memory of a long lost love and the realization that he's probably alive somewhere and looking for her too. She begins the quest to find him and right the wrong so many years ago.

Who is he? What wrong do they have to make right?

263. Your heroine is dreaming. She's flying through the air, smiling and heading to a specific destination. She gets there, puts her feet on the ground and there's an unfamiliar man standing there as if he's waiting for her. The man is real and is also somewhere sleeping and sharing her dream. Who is he? Where are they?

264. Your heroine is a bartender. She's heard it all, seen it all and done most of it too. One night (maybe during a full moon on Halloween when everyone is dressed up and emotions are heightened) she meets someone she'll never forget.

He tells her a secret over a drink. What is he drinking? What does he tell her? How does it change her life?

265. How would your heroine react if she found a notebook that made people die? What would she do with it and why?

266. Have you ever had a dream that inspired you to write a story?

Your heroine is having creepy dreams. They're so creepy that she's compelled to write them down. The writing is partially therapeutic. However, when she writes it is almost as if she is in a trance, as if someone is writing through her.

Start your story with her writing. What is she experiencing? Who is haunting her and why?

For example, maybe she's being haunted by a woman who wants to reunite with her lover who is still alive. The dreams lead your heroine to seek out this lover and maybe they start something romantic. Then your heroine has to deal with an angry ghost!

267. Your heroine is on a hot air balloon ride. She's celebrating. The balloon starts to go down. What happens?

268. Do you believe in magic? Start your story here – a young woman walks upon a man casting a spell in the woods. She's camping with friend, not walking in the woods alone at night – TSTL. Why is he casting a spell and what does he do when she catches him?

269. Your heroine owns and creates a line of special bath products. She makes them for each client individually based on their needs.

For example, if a woman is pining for a man who just won't commit then she mixes up bath salts or body wash with a little something extra to make him realize the error of his ways.

A very sexy and very angry man bursts into her shop accusing her of ruining his life. What does she do? What did she do to ruin his life?

270. Your heroine is a fairy which means she likes to cause trouble. When she falls for a special someone the tables are turned because this time he's the one causing the trouble. What happens?

271. An angel must save the life of a man/woman they hate. Why do they hate them? What's the history and how do they turn it around? What happens?

272. Your heroine is a Funeral Director who talks to ghosts. Yes, she sees dead people and when one of them pleads for her help to protect their brother, she's compelled to help. Especially when he's the sexiest man she's ever laid eyes on. What happens? What does she need to protect him from?

273. A tattoo artist is also a witch. She likes to put a little magic into every tattoo to help her clients, her magic went a little too far with one of her clients and he wants revenge. What did she do and how did her magic get carried away?

274. Your heroine is a Greek goddess reincarnated. A Greek god she wronged as a goddess is still sour and bent on revenge. Which goddess is she and what Greek god is after her? What man enters her life and helps her come to grips on her past?

275. Your heroine is the willing host to an alien life form. However, unlike Sigourney Weaver in Aliens, she has become attached to the being. She can hear his thoughts, feel his feelings and she's strangely attracted to him. Why is

she a host to him and what happens? How do they get together?

276. Your heroine has a spirit attached to her. It's not evil; instead it's just part of her life. It seems to essentially live off of her. One day when the spirit is particularly distracting she literally bumps into a man who can see the spirit too.

He calls them "energy leeches" and explains to her that only people who have certain extraordinary qualities have spirit leeches. He invites her to join an elite team of spiritual warriors who can use their power to fight crime. Who is she and what does she decide to do?

277. Your heroine is a dog trainer who actually hears their thoughts and can sense their emotions. What does she do when a dog starts talking back to her? Why can he hear and understand her, and what happens?

278. Your heroine is in a horrible accident. She wakes to find herself in a foreign land (Alien? Time travel?) with a handsome stranger at her side. He too was in an accident. What brought them together and how do they get back to their lives (or are they actually dead)?

279. Your heroine is a werewolf. There aren't many female werewolves and thus it is her responsibility to keep the clan thriving. To do so she must mate with their leader. Unfortunately, he's a jerk and she's less than attracted to him.

She meets another werewolf from a rival pack and falls instantly in love. But, her commitment to her clan's survival gets in the way of their being together – not to mention he's supposed to be her mortal enemy. How does she resolve her conflict? (Think Romeo and Juliet only with werewolves!)

280. They say you can see a person's soul through their eyes. For your heroine this is completely true. She can not only see their soul, but also their past lives. She meets a man and realizes their souls are connected. Who is he and what happens?

281. Your hero and heroine are magicians. Actually, your heroine is a magician's assistant. They're immortal and have been performing their act for centuries, changing their persona and their act with the times.

Until one day your hero pulls a different assistant from the audience. Who is she? What happens? Why is he drawn to her and how does his old assistant handle the betrayal?

282. 423 years ago your hero saw your heroine kill his mother. They both hold in their possession devices that help them travel through time, and your hero has been chasing her through time ever since.

Now he's crafted a trap. How will he capture her and what happens when he does? Why did she kill his mother?

283. A landscape designer talks to plants. She's actually a nature fairy/witch and has power over nature. Someone or something has poisoned the plants in her domain and she is bent on finding out what is going on.

Her research leads her to a man. Who is he? What does he have to do with the dying plants? If he's not behind their death, who is and why?

284. A woman is bitten by a dog. She then turns into a dog. Wandering around she goes to the places that are familiar to her, like her boyfriend's home. She sees him cheating on her. She takes off and is found by a man who cares for her. What happens that turns her back into a human and what does her newfound "owner" do about it?

285. Voodoo runs deep in your heroine's family history, yet she wants nothing to do with the black magic until something significant happens. What happens? Why does she turn to the magic? Who does she turn to and what happens?

286. A meteor has hit earth. It has devastated your heroine. As she tries to survive in this chaos a new society emerges. It's a rough and lawless one where the rich thrive and the poor suffer.

She meets a man who leads a team of contractors. They're not government sanctioned and a bit rough around the edges, but deep down their goals are to help others less fortunate rebuild. How do they band together? What happens?

287. Your heroine and hero grew up together. A hatred for something horrible bonded them for life. Now they've eliminated that thing from the world. Without a purpose, they're left to face the feelings that have been building between them.

What do they do? Start the story with them delivering the final blow to their nemesis. (This could easily be a historical romance, paranormal or even an urban fantasy.)

288. Your heroine was promised to the reaper by her mother. Her mother made the deal in order to save her

lover. Now your heroine is approaching her 25th birthday and the day she's supposed to marry the reaper. How does she get out of the deal?

289. Your heroine gets a mysterious package in the mail. She opens it and something strange happens…what happens?

290. Your heroine needs to capture a demon to fulfill her family obligations and finally be free. Now she has her demon. What does she do with him?

291. A paranormal investigator is surprised when she investigates a house known for a brutal murder. The owner, a handsome house flipper, is dedicated to giving the home a new history. The past may have other ideas. What does she find when she investigates?

292. Your heroine sometimes dreams about things before they happen. It hasn't happened in a long time. Long enough that she's almost forgotten about it. Until today. What happens? What did she dream?

293. Your heroine is surfing. She catches a dream wave and then the unthinkable happens. She falls off her board and gets smacked in the head. As she's going down under the water she sees something strange. What does she see?

294. Your heroine inherits a bar from a long lost relative in a small town somewhere in Europe. The bar is abandoned and she's excited about fixing it up and starting a new life. She's there late one night fixing it up and is visited by a ghost. Who visits her and what does she do?

295. Your hero or heroine is walking past a sidewalk chalk artist who has drawn a 3D image. When they step on the

image they're instantly inside it. Where are they and what happens next?

296. Your hero is dreaming that he's flying. He wakes up, but he's not in his bed. Where is he and how did he get there?

297. Your heroine dreams she's being eaten by a wolf then wakes up to find….

298. Your heroine opens a door and finds herself in a land where the earth has dried up and there are only two remaining civilizations – one of only men and one of only women.

The women strive to keep the men out of their city. Any men that sneak in become slaves. Your heroine falls for one of the slaves. What happens next? Does she try to get home? Does she stay?

299. Your hero has been wrongfully imprisoned (on another planet?). He escapes and is on the run. Who does he meet? What happens?

300. Four sisters – each is one of the natural elements of the northern hemisphere; earth, wind, fire and water. What happens when they meet their male counterparts in the southern hemisphere?

301. Five reputable paranormal investigators are invited to investigate the notorious haunting of a mansion/ranch/plantation/hotel (you decide). It's the anniversary of a horrific accident/murder that occurred there more than 100 years ago. What happens to the investigators? What do they discover?

302. A sexy horror writer takes residence in your heroine's bed and breakfast. He's there until he finishes his novel. When someone dies, all clues point to him.

303. Your heroine uncovers a Mayan artifact that has magical powers. What is it and what can it do?

304. A romance writer falls in love with her muse. Is her muse alive or imaginary? What does she do about her infatuation? How does her muse respond?

305. Your heroine is at a company party at a local hotel that is rumored to be haunted. She has too much to drink and falls asleep. What wakes her up?

306. Your hero is able to see all the lies and mistakes a person is made by touching their feet. He avoids touching people's feet (which isn't too difficult) because knowing what a person has done is too much information. However, when he meets a mystery woman he cannot resist. What does he learn?

307. Remember the television show "Isis" from the early 1970's? Your heroine is Isis reincarnated. How does she find out who she is?

308. Your heroine moves into an old abandoned home. She's determined to fix it up – it's a metaphor for fixing up her own life, which is in shambles. She inadvertently releases a ghost who wants her dead because her death would free the ghost from the home. How does your heroine survive?

309. Your heroine is hunkering down in her home during a snowstorm. She pulls on her coat and boots to get more

firewood. Outside she swears she sees a yeti run past. She chases after him. What happens next?

310. Your heroine is on a tour of an old home. She looks at a picture hanging on the wall and sees her own face staring back. She passes out from shock and wakes not in the past, but in the future. Who is she and what happens next?

311. Looking at the sky, your protagonist begins to see faces form in the clouds. They speak to him. What do they say?

312. Your heroine's new boyfriend is wonderful. She's in love. But, his ex-girlfriend is a real bitch; she's a fairy and she wants him back. That means she has some ugly tricks up her sleeve. Good thing your heroine has a few tricks of her own.

313. Your heroine has a secret weapon. Her shoes – magic shoes – uncoil into venomous snakes that strike lightening fast. Start your story as their silvery bodies begin unwinding themselves from around her ankles.

314. Your heroine receives a blood transfusion and beings having nightmares, cravings and is behaving strangely. What happened? Whose blood did she receive?

315. Your heroine is a nurse. She's been transferred to a new hospital and almost immediately begins seeing ghosts. Why and what happens?

316. Your heroine is a dragon trainer. She's the best in the world until she meets your hero and he challenges her on every level. What happens the first time they meet?

317. Your hero is a merman, yep, he lives in the sea. His race is dying and he needs to find your heroine. Who is she? How does he find her?

318. Your heroine is a witch. She doesn't practice publicly and keeps her skills to herself. Yet when two men come to her – each with an opposing curse – she must decide which one to help.

319. Your hero was born with the task of finding an artifact before his 29th birthday. He turns 29 in two weeks and hasn't found the artifact yet. If he fails, he dies. What happens?

320. Your heroine is half fairy and half human. Her parentage makes it possible for her to live in both worlds. She uses her abilities to solve crimes committed by fae in the human world and vice versa. During an investigation she uncovers a fae plot to take over the human world. What happens?

321. Your heroine is half fairy and half human, and someone wants her dead. One by one other half breeds like her are being killed off. Your heroine's time is running short. What does she do to stay alive? Who helps her?

322. Your heroine is a big city homicide detective. When a dead body is found in an alley it looks as if the brain has been eaten. More and more bodies pile up and she begins to think they have a zombie on their hands. But, zombies don't exist, right?

323. Your hero has been possessed. Instead of exorcising the demon from his body he decides to use it to help him finally kill the demon drug lord that killed his family. But,

his new partner isn't so excited about his agenda or the demon inside him.

324. Your heroine is a witch. As her fellow coven members begin to disappear she must convince the local police chief to investigate. The first step, however, is to convince him that witches are real and not fairy tale fantasies. How does she convince him?

325. Your hero is charged with the task of killing a renegade werewolf. He finds the werewolf with a woman. She appears to be the wolf's victim. He isn't sure. After killing the wolf he takes the woman with him. She's been bitten and needs a transfusion to survive. Is she to be trusted?

326. Your heroine works in a bed and breakfast in Gettysburg. Every day she has to dress like a civil war nurse and pretend. Yet something in the old building doesn't think she's pretending.

She makes contact with the ghost of a long lost nurse who used to work in the very same building. Your heroine digs and realizes the heroine died the night before she was to wed.

Thinking that re-enacting the wedding that she should have had might free the spirit from the home, your heroine finds an old family member from the spirit's groom's family. He's her age and he's good looking to boot. How does she convince him to go along with her ghostly reenactment?

327. Your hero realizes that he has a super power. He can control stoplights by blinking his eyes or something – you can choose the superpower. However, your hero uses his powers for bad. He controls the lights so he doesn't have to

stop, ever. He misuses his power. Until he realizes that his actions have caused someone harm. For example, maybe a woman had to wait at a light and ended up not making it to the hospital in time to say goodbye to her mother. What happens?

328. Your hero comes across a woman's skeleton. He disturbs it. What happens next?

329. Your hero sees a little girl drain the blood of a homeless person and leave the body in an alley. What happens next?

330. Your heroine is psychic and helps others by solving crimes and finding missing loved ones. She's attacked and hit over the head. The injury causes her to lose her abilities just when she needs them most. Who is after her?

331. Your heroine's mother has tortured and controlled her for years. She's been promised her freedom if she does one last task. What is it?

332. Your heroine takes a glassblowing class and discovers she has some unusual abilities. What happens?

333. Your heroine sees someone standing on the railroad tracks and a train is bearing down on them. She rushes to their aid, but just as the train approaches the person disappears.

As she is rushing to the person's aid a man is coming to help her. He too sees the person disappear. What happens next?

334. Your heroine is in a car accident and wakes up underground. She has died and the king that lives below the

earth revived her and stole her from her grave. What happens when she discovers that she has died?

335. St Patrick's Day is your hero's least favorite day. For a cop In Boston it means chaos and tons of drunken idiots. Boy is he surprised when he sees a leprechaun darting across the street, he's even more surprised by the woman chasing the leprechaun. Who is she?

336. Your heroine is a florist who discovers a never before seen flower in her greenhouse. What does she do with it?

337. Your heroine is pregnant. Trouble is, she hasn't been with anyone in a very long time. If you don't count her dreams, that is. So how did she get pregnant?

338. Your hero is a warlock with significant power, both magically and politically. He's used to women throwing themselves at him. Yet when he meets your heroine he's taken aback that she's not the least bit interested in him. Why isn't she interested in him?

339. Your hero is preparing for an epic battle. As part of the prep he needs..?

340. Your hero is dead. He killed himself to save his love. He finds himself standing over his own grave with no memory except her face. What happens?

341. Your heroine has been captured and tortured because of her unique abilities. What can she do and why do they want her?

342. Your hero or heroine is about to practice death magic. Why? What happens?

343. Your heroine is working at a blood drive. Someone wants to give blood and she tries to turn him away. Why?

344. Your hero is a photographer and a demon or vampire hunter (you decide who or what he's hunting). He can tell if they're otherworldly when he looks at them through his camera. What happens when he finally sees his love interest through his lens?

345. Your hero is a fallen angel. He has just fallen and is still in shock. What made him fall?

346. Determined to marry off their sister, a group of well-intentioned family witches concoct a brew to help your heroine attract a husband. Their spell goes badly. What or who does your heroine attract?

347. Your heroine is drawn to a voodoo priest, she doesn't believe the attraction is anything other than one of his spells, or curses. How does he convince/seduce her?

348. Your hero falls down a manhole and discovers a whole new world. What does he first see when he falls down the hole?

349. The Moors have a reputation of being haunted. Your hero goes to the Moors to study and uncovers a deep dark secret. What happens?

350. Your heroine is one of a small team of people headed to a planet that has gone out of control. Their job? To restore order. What happens when your heroine meets the lead anarchist?

351. The waters are rising and a storm has been predicted – this final storm will wipe out the last of civilization unless…

352. Someone is burning witches in the woods of a small rural community and your heroine might be next. What does she do to save her own life?

353. Your heroine is seeking the man known only as the "Device Maker." Who is he and why is she searching for him?

354. Your heroine is visiting the Acropolis. Standing there outside this amazing structure when she has a vision and remembers who she is. Who is she?

355. Your heroine is a nurse who sees, literally sees, a patient's soul leave their body when they die. She also sees an angel in the room. When the angel realizes he can be seen by her, what happens?

356. Your heroine wakes to find sparrows falling from the sky onto her lawn. What is causing this to happen and what does she do about it?

357. Your heroine is taking her morning jog through the woods when she hears the trees talking. What are they saying and why can she hear them?

358. Your hero/heroine is lying on the floor and sees an eyeball in the ceiling. It's looking down at them. Why?

359. Only your heroine can stop the pending Armageddon. What does she do first when she realizes it's all up to her?

360. Your heroine has led her people to defeat an overthrow of her planet. To do so she turned her back on

her upbringing. Now she must pay the price. What is the price?

361. Your hero or heroine has been turned into a vampire or werewolf or something else – you decide. They fight their way to see a wise man or prophet who knows a way they can become human again. What do they have to do?

362. Your heroine is being haunted by the ghost of a witch who was burned at the stake by a religious zealot. To make things right, and get rid of the crazy ghost, she must find the bones of the other victims and perform a ceremony. How does she get started? Who helps her? Start your story with her meeting the ghost witch for the first time.

363. Your heroine is convinced that her boyfriend is possessed. What does she do?

364. Your heroine is conducting a study on the cultural phenomenon of "Love Manga." She's reading a Love Manga book when suddenly she's inside the pages and part of the story. What happens?

365. Your heroine is sitting on the hood of her car enjoying the nighttime stars when she sees something she is certain is a UFO. What does she do?

366. Your heroine is a fairy, but she stinks at being one. She needs a tutor and the only person willing to help her out is the person she hates the most. Why is he willing to help her? Why does she hate him?

367. Your heroine is a photo journalist and has been assigned the task of taking photos inside a historic, and abandoned, house. The house is rumored to be haunted by family that was murdered there more than fifty years ago.

She's terrified, but not willing to risk her reputation or her career by chickening out. She pushes open the creaky door of the house and....what happens next?

368. Your hero is walking through the woods. He's wearing a red hoodie. He comes upon a …..

369. Your heroine is in a taxicab with another passenger. They're involved in an accident and they both die. Now they're bound together for all eternity and they're assigned a task that they must complete, together, before they're allowed to transcend. What must they do?

370. Your hero is being haunted by two women. Why?

371. Your hero/heroine hears a whisper in a dream. The whisper says, "Come to the edge, he said. They said: We are afraid. Come to the edge, he said. They came. He pushed them, and they flew..." Your hero/heroine then finds themselves at the edge of a cliff. What do they do?

372. Your heroine discovered the "Other Side" as a child. At a sleepover with a friend they wrote on a mirror. When they awoke, there was an answer to their question written backwards in the mirror – someone on the other side answered.

From that point on she's always known there was something more. Today, as she's standing in front of a mirror, she sees someone on the other side. Who is he and what does she do?

373. Your hero and heroine are tied together at the top of a thirty foot column. Why?

374. Your heroine is a doctor. She discovers that a patient has two hearts. One is beating loud and strong, the other appears to be a phantom heart. It's there, but it's not attached to anything in his body — yet it beats. Who is the patient and what does your heroine do?

375. Your hero suddenly has someone inside his head. They're talking to him. What are they saying? Who are they? How is your hero reacting?

376. Your heroine's toy has been talking to her since she was a child. It has helped her manage her difficult life. Now her toy is gone. What does she do?

377. Your hero or heroine is sitting at the family dinner table. They're traveling in a different country and is the guest of a large farming family. They hear heavy, insistent, pounding on the door.

No one gets up. Everyone just looks at each other, surprised. It's late at night. The pounding continues. Finally, the grandmother gets up and answers the door. There's no one there. The wind blows something in. What does it blow in?

378. Your hero or heroine has the opportunity to change one moment in their life. How did they get that opportunity and what do they do with it?

379. Your heroine has had enough. Someone cuts in line at the grocery and she flips out. What happens?

380. Your heroine comes across some magic words. What are they and what does she do with them?

381. Your heroine is on a cross-country train when she meets a mysterious and somewhat amusing man. The train is stopped, but the robbers don't want money, they want this man and your heroine gets caught up in the adventure. What happens?

382. Your heroine gets a message from the future. What does it say? What does she do?

383. Your hero just died. He has a very important message to get to someone. It's urgent. What is the message and how does he deliver it?

384. When your hero/heroine was a child they were visited by a "monster." Assuming it was just in their imagination, his/her parents dismissed it. Eventually, the monster went away. now it's back. Why?

385. Your heroine agrees to join a friend and a few others (all strangers to her) in a dare – the goal is to spend a full night in one of the most haunted places in the country. What happens?

386. Your hero hires a team of ghost hunters to dispel the myth that his bar is haunted. He's not prepared for the leader of the team or her findings. What happens?

387. From the outside your cute heroine may look like a crazy cat lady. She has a home full of them. However, they're not really cats, they're her family. How did they become cats? What is she going to do about it?

388. Your heroine, a demigoddess, has been ordered to replace a man's wife and bear him a child. She has no choice. The gods have "removed" his wife, your heroine is

in place, once she gets to know him, can she continue with the deception?

389. Your heroine is forced to take over her mother's "medicine woman" practice while she recovers in the hospital. She doesn't believe in the practices her mother follows, learns a lot about the people around her and discovers love in an unusual place. What happens?

390. When the oracle tells your heroine her future is bound to your hero, she laughs out loud. Then she cries. Knowing that the oracle has told your hero the same thing, she heads out to confront him. She wants to set the record straight; "Their future is not together." What happens?

391. Your heroine is hiding in the shadows as she watches a group of men prepare to hunt – people. With the words "let us prey" they head out and she decides to follow them. What happens?

392. Your hero has been raised by his uncle and father to take over the "business." But on the evening of his acceptance into the business he discovers one of the victims affected by their cruel reign.

Can he fulfill his birthright or will he join the rebellion and follow his heart? "Family business" can mean anything from mafia to interplanetary governmental control. You decide where and when this story takes place and what the family business is.

393. Your heroine and her sister have ruled together for years. What happens when she finds love and is forced to choose between love and the power she was groomed for?

394. Your heroine possesses the ability to borrow the powers of other creatures. For example, she can be a necromancer for a while or possess the powers of a fairy. Someone has discovered her ability and wants to use her for their own purposes. And someone wants to protect her. Who? What happens?

395. Your hero just moved in with his girlfriend. She lives in an old home that used to be part of the Underground Railroad. They're a mixed race couple and once he moves in, strange things begin happening in the home. Start your story with move-in day. What happens?

396. Your hero has been cursed. Why? Who cursed him and what does he do about it?

397. Your heroine is a witch, a good witch. She's dating a new man and someone else, another witch, wants him. Bad things start happening to your heroine almost immediately. Start your story with one of these unfortunate events. What happens?

398. Your heroine is a succubus who doesn't want to be one. She uses her powers for good. How? What does she do?

399. Your heroine's boat crashes on an island. The island is inhabited by a magician and his son. Your heroine is the first person they've seen in many years. What happens?

400. Your heroine is an inventor. She's invented an underwater boat that can stay submerged for ten full days. Others want her boat for nefarious reasons. Why? What does she do? Who helps her?

Notes:

Chapter 4

Romantic Suspense, Mystery

401. Your heroine wakes from a very vivid dream in which her dead mother or grandmother asks her to find an old family heirloom. She begins her quest to find the object and enlists her neighbor's help – he's known her family for decades.

Her neighbor's son offers to help and together the two of them search. What is she looking for and where do they find it?

402. Your heroine is on the run from a drug kingpin. She accidentally overheard a conversation and now holds the key to his ruin. He won't stop until she's caught. She's quickly captured by a thug, only he isn't who he appears. He's an undercover cop/agent. What is their first interaction like and how do they bring the drug kingpin down?

403. Your heroine's daughter is snatched from her bedroom in the middle of the night. Is it a case of a teenager running away or is something more nefarious at play?

A handsome detective helps your heroine find the answers, and her daughter. What is their first interaction like and how do they manage the instant attraction amidst potential tragedy?

404. Your heroine is new to town and when her power goes out she runs next door to borrow a flashlight, only to find

her neighbor being held at gunpoint. It's a classic case of being in the wrong place at the wrong time....what happens next?

405. A used bookstore owner is left speechless when her favorite author, a rugged outdoorsman who writes survival stories, walks in the door.

After several consecutive visits to her store she finally manages to hold a normal conversation with him. He invites her for lunch at his cabin, but what starts out as a normal date quickly turns into a real life survival story when...What happens?

406. Your heroine wakes one morning with a tattoo on her body. She doesn't know where she got it or why. Even more mysterious, is the tattoo itself. What is it? Who gave it to her and why?

407. A small town bakery is vandalized and the new sheriff is on the job.

He puts extra effort into finding the vandal when he meets your heroine and the owner of the bakery. Not only does she make the best baked goods he's ever eaten, she's cute and newly single. Who is vandalizing her bakery and why is she newly single?

408. Your heroine has just survived something that terrified her. In response to it she craves the normalcy of household chores. In the midst of a cleaning frenzy she is cleaning out the vents in her home.

Reaching in, she finds..? What caused your heroine to want to escape and find normalcy in household chores? What does she find inside the walls of her home?

For example, maybe she wakes in the middle of the night to find an intruder in her home. He's searching for something. He knocks her down, but not before she gets a good look at his eyes – otherworldly eyes.

The next day, she's cleaning and finds a box with ancient writing on the top of it. Inside the box are an old cameo necklace and the picture of a man with otherworldly eyes.

409. Now imagine your heroine on a hiking trail. She is bitten by a rattlesnake and she is by herself. What does she do? Does someone come along who helps her?

Does she drag her poison filled body to the trailhead, which is of course many miles away? Does a handsome vet, doc, or firefighter come to her aid?

410. Your heroine is a paramedic. She's used to difficult situations, high stress and ugly surprises. But, nothing surprises her more than when she shows up to an emergency scene and finds her ex.

A man, once the love of her life who she's never really gotten over, and who is supposed to be dead. What happens? Why is he hurt? How does he explain the fact that he's alive and where has he been all this time? Why did he let her think he was dead? How does she react when she sees him?

411. What mystery lies in the woods in a deep dark hole? Why is this hole here? Who dug it? What secrets does it contain?

412. Your hero, an FBI operative, finds herself the target of a stalker. The profiler assigned to help her identify the stalker is someone she's never really liked. To say they

don't get along would be putting it mildly. How will they work together to find her stalker before she becomes a victim and how will they be able to work together despite their animosity – and attraction?

413. There's something odd about the new guy in your heroine's cooking class. Fancying herself an amateur sleuth, she decides to find out what his story is. When he catches her spying on him, all bets are off. What does she catch him doing?

414. Your heroine is a search and rescue volunteer in the mountains of Colorado. Her summer days are often filled with rescuing climbers from peaks or rock faces and her winters are spent searching for lost hikers, skiers and snowmobilers. What happens to her to strand her in the wilderness, who finds her and what happens next?

415. Your heroine's best friend is missing, and while her friend is known to have some wild escapades she never turns her phone off. But, this time there's no getting a hold of her. After five days of worrying, she finally decides to call a one night stand she had several months ago for help.

416. Your hero is a former marine and private investigator, and when your heroine shows up on his doorstep looking for answers about a missing friend, he's compelled to help her. What's happened to her friend and how do these two hook up?

417. Your heroine runs a firm that helps parents whose children have been abducted navigate the legal system. She also offers support and help in understanding the best strategies to dealing with the police, the media, and how to find their child quickly.

A victim of abduction as a child, she knows the effect the media and the legal system can have on a family. When an unusual case, one that closely resembles her own, comes into her life she must turn to an ex for help before it's too late for a little girl.

418. Your heroine has a bad temper. She's a top level executive who is just plain old burnt out. On the way to a client meeting her plane crashes. She and the pilot survive.

They're alone in the mountains without anyone or anything – a forced "vacation" and a wakeup call about where her life is going. What does she learn and how does the pilot (whom she's really nasty to at first) help her?

419. A soap opera star is in the midst of an intense stalker story line when she finds herself being stalked in real life. A police officer, your hero, is assigned her case and while he definitely has the hots for her, he's also convinced she's a drama queen and he doesn't completely believe her story about being stalked. How does she convince him?

420. A prosecutor ticks off a mob boss. She's assigned a bodyguard, but in a case where everyone is a suspect can she trust him with her life? What happens? How is she convinced he can be trusted?

421. A woman on the run finds $500,000. What happens? Who does it belong to? Why is she on the run?

422. Your heroine takes folks out for helicopter ski trips. When an avalanche wipes out most of her group it's up to her to save a father and his son. While they're fighting to stay alive they just might fall in love.

423. Your hero and heroine are in a survival situation in an airplane. What's the situation? Who are your characters and how do they meet/connect?

424. When your hero, a sheriff, finds a woman asleep in her car on the side of the road he assumes she's drunk., she's not; she's beautiful and in trouble. Who is she and what trouble is she in?

425. Your heroine's sister was murdered and your heroine will stop at nothing to get revenge. Until she meets your hero and he's just as determined to stop her. Why? Who is he? Does he stop her or does she convince him to join her?

426. Your heroine is sailing a ship around the world. It's an extreme reaction to a traumatic event in her life. Along her journey, no doubt in a remote and paradise-like setting, she meets a man.

He helps her overcome her trauma and find the life and the love she's been seeking all along. What happens to your heroine to make her take such a dramatic journey? Who does she meet and how does he help her?

427. Your heroine's brother was murdered. Now she'll stop at nothing to find out who killed him. Her quest for justice gets her up close and personal with the murderer. Will she find out who it is before it's too late? Who killed her brother and why?

428. Your heroine is a detective who has been hired to find a man. She doesn't know why, but she knows the paycheck will help her get out from under. She hits the road in search of this man. Where does she find him? Who is he? What happens?

429. Your heroine is being stalked and no one believes her. What does she do? Who is stalking her?

430. Your heroine's father is missing. He has been gone for months. In less than one week he'll be declared legally dead and her step mother will inherit everything. She heads out on one final attempt to find her dad. Her spaceship/car/airplane/time travel device crashes. Where does she wake up? Is there anyone with her when she wakes?

431. Your heroine is a cop. She's returned to the backwoods community she grew up in to help solve a case. She's teamed up with a city slicker type who just can't handle the local folks. Start your story with their first conversation in the patrol car heading to a crime scene or to talk to witnesses.

432. Your hero is doing repairs on your heroine's house when he finds a human skeleton. What does he do? Does he turn her into the police? Does he start investigating her? Does he confront her?

433. Your heroine is on her way to an urgent meeting/appointment. She's driving in a wicked storm and power lines fall onto her car. She's trapped and terrified, what happens next?

434. An off duty firefighter/cop helps to deliver a baby. He hands the baby to the doctor/EMT. When he turns around, the mother is gone. What does he do? Where did she go?

435. Your heroine marries a man because he is able to help her cause. He has a lot of money and while she doesn't love him, she likes him and the community she cares about desperately needs financial assistance. He's not who she

thinks he is. He's bad. What does he do and how does she get away? Start the story as she's trying to escape him.

436. Your heroine is a writer. She writes mystery novels. Her latest novel is capturing headlines, only they're not the kind of headlines she wants.

Someone is murdered exactly like the murder in her latest book. Unfortunately, the murder was committed before she wrote her book. Now she's the prime suspect.

437. Your heroine, a physical therapist, goes undercover to prove a wealthy bachelor killed her sister. Start your story with her first encounter with him. He's not what she expected.

438. Your heroine's sister disappears minutes before she's supposed to get married. What does she do?

439. Your heroine is a pilot. While out on a flying lesson the plane crashes. What happens to her handsome student?

440. Your heroine finds lost children. It's her life's mission and the foundation of her investigation company. When the niece of a millionaire is missing your hero puts himself in the middle of her investigation. The two have opposing viewpoints on how to find the missing child. Start your story with the first time they meet – their first interaction.

441. After a personal hardship, your heroine moves back into her childhood home. She discovers a body buried in the backyard and must solve the mystery. Who is buried in the grave and how did they die?

442. Your Southern belle heroine wakes to find a dead body in her front yard. She won't be satisfied until the

hunky detective assigned to the case finds out who he is and why he died.

443. Your hero knows that his friend's helicopter training accident was anything but. It was murder and he's determined to find out who killed him, and why. First stop, the person running the training. He expects to find a hardnosed military man, instead he finds a stubborn and sexy woman. What happens next?

444. Your hero is a police detective that is assigned to question a female photographer whose recent photos depict violent murders. The subjects of the photos bear an eerie resemblance to photos of missing women. Does she know these women? Are the photos real or staged?

445. Your heroine is on the run from an abusive boyfriend. She's hiding on a Colorado ranch and sleeping in the barn when the rancher discovers her. He's not amused, but he is attracted. What happens next?

446. Your heroine is a firefighter. While fighting a five alarm fire she gets smacked over the head – someone is trying to kill her. How does she get out alive and what happens next?

447. Your heroine is camping with her boyfriend. They fight and he takes off (yep, he's a jerk) so she's left alone in the woods. What happens?

448. Your protagonist is eating Chinese takeout alone in their apartment. They open the fortune cookie expecting to see a trite cliché and a few lucky numbers. Instead they get…

449. Your heroine is a hostage negotiator, but she's unable to talk down a woman who takes her child with her in a murder/suicide. Ten years later she encounters the widower. He doesn't know the role she's played in his past. What happens?

450. Your heroine owns a second hand store. When she shows up one morning she finds a box on her doorstep. What is inside?

451. Your heroine is in a bar when a bullet goes through the beer bottle she's holding. She turns around and sees someone holding a gun aimed right at her. Who is it and what does she do?

452. Your heroine is a club singer. It's a cover for her real job and provides her with the perfect opportunity to keep an eye on... What is her real job and who or what does she need to keep an eye on?

453. Your heroine owns a vintage jewelry store. When a piece of stolen merchandise lands in her store, she must find out who it belongs to in order to clear her name. Who does the jewelry belong to and how does she find them?

454. Your heroine is a crime writer who is on hard times. She needs money, bad. She sets her sights on a notoriously evasive criminal and finds herself caught in his web and questioning everything she ever believed in. What happens?

455. When your heroine was a child she and her entire family were kidnapped and used as guinea pigs for the genetic experiments of a mad man. Only she escaped and survived. Now she's pregnant and on the run. What happens?

456. Your heroine inherited a bed and breakfast in a weird town. When she arrives half the town is excited to see her – a little too excited – and the other half is looking at her like she's an alien from another planet, including the handsome handyman standing on her porch. What happens? What makes the town and their reaction to her so strange?

457. Your heroine is out of town for work. She stops at a gas station and ends up in a hostage situation with strangers. She misses her plane and her rental car is destroyed. A fellow hostage offers his couch. What happens next?

458. Your heroine is an endurance runner. She joins an adventure racing team. As the only female she feels like it's her responsibility to be tougher than the others. That's pretty hard to do, especially when you're attracted to one of your team members.

What happens during their first race when their endurance is really tested? Start your story at a point in the race when she feels like she has to quit or die.

459. Your heroine is camping with friends when one of them disappears. They find her in an abandoned mineshaft facing the wall and rocking back and forth. Something terrible has happened. What?

460. Your hero is driving down the road one night and comes across a naked woman stumbling down the street. He pulls over and wraps her in a blanket. She seems confused. Smartly, he calls the cops, but when he turns around she's gone. She turns up dead and has his blanket with her. What happened?

461. Your heroine is an acupuncturist. Her patient has just died on the table. Now what?

462. Your heroine finds a gun stashed under her filing cabinet. It doesn't belong to her. Who does it belong to?

463. Your hero stashes a gun under his doctor's filing cabinet. Why does he have a gun (and why does he need to hide it)? Why does he choose this hiding place?

464. Your heroine is an undercover cop assigned to infiltrate a girl gang and find out who killed a local teen.

465. Your hero is on the coast on a construction/contracting job that will make or break his business. A hurricane hits and threatens not only his potential success, but also his life and the lives of his employees. What happens?

466. Your heroine put a man in jail and now she needs his help. Why?

467. Your heroine has rented a small boat with friends and is enjoying her vacation when they're boarded by pirates. What happens next?

468. Your hero and heroine are both in the wrong place at the wrong time. A volcano is erupting. What happens?

469. Hot on the trail of a thief, your hero discovers it's a woman he's been lusting after for years. What happens next? What did she steal?

470. Your heroine is the Dean of Admissions at a small college. When a young student goes on a shooting spree your heroine becomes part of the investigation and teams up with a new teacher to find out what went wrong.

471. Your heroine is an ESL (English as a Second Language) teacher. When her favorite student disappears she's afraid that agents from U.S. Citizenship and Immigrations Services grabbed her. She starts digging and enlists the help of your hero. Who is he and what does he do? What happened to her student?

472. Your hero is the right hand man for a corporate whiz. He's tired of getting the short end of the stick. He wants a bit of recognition. What does he do?

473. Your hero or heroine is out for a walk. They see an apple in a tree and climb up to get it. They get stuck. Now what?

474. Everyone keeps telling your hero he looks like a certain celebrity. He finally snaps. Who does he look like and what happens when he snaps?

475. Your heroine is sitting in her car reading a book when she sees a car pull up and snatch a young girl. She's the only witness to the incident. How does she help the cops and a single dad get the girl back?

476. Your heroine is a cleaner upper. She cleans up her bosses messes to ensure that his image and the company image stay untarnished. When her boss's kid does something awful she has to make a decision; should she clean the mess up or let it, and her job, go? What happens and what did the boss's kid do?

477. Your hero is a talk show host. He's being stalked by a woman. What happens when she corners him and he can't get away?

478. Your hero notices a woman being bothered by a fellow bus passenger. What does he do?

479. Your heroine has just landed her dream job only to learn that the previous five people in that job died untimely (and suspicious) deaths. What happens?

480. Your hero or heroine owns a bar in a small town. Someone wants the bar closed and is sabotaging it. Start your story with their first serious sabotaging effort. What happens?

481. Egyptian artifacts are being stolen from museums. Your heroine is determined to find out who is behind the thefts and why. What happens when she discovers who the thief is?

482. Your hero or heroine is the owner of a local newspaper. When the townspeople's secrets start making the front page anonymously, your protagonist faces a conundrum.

Do they find out who is leaking the scandalous secrets before their own family secrets are revealed or do they stay out of it and continue enjoying the profits the anonymous reporter is bringing in?

483. Someone is killing women and leaving Christmas decorations stolen from their yard with the body. Your heroine is next on the list. How does your detective/police officer hero protect her?

484. Your heroine's job is to get in and out of top restaurants and review them. It's all fine until someone tries to kill her. The police suspect a local restaurateur; she gave them a bad review. What happens?

485. Your heroine loves shoes and suddenly it seems she has a shoe fairy. Each morning when she wakes up she finds a new pair of designer shoes in her closet. She sets a trap to find out who is leaving her the shoes. What happens?

486. To stop human trafficking, your heroine has gone undercover in a motorcycle gang that is rumored to be deeply involved in local activities. She passes the first initiation. What does she have to do to pass the second initiation?

487. Your heroine is an agent who was captured and brainwashed. After being rescued she's ready to get back to the job – trouble is she keeps blacking out and finding herself in strange situations. Start your story with her awaking and being in one such situation. Where is she and what happens?

488. Your heroine is convinced her boyfriend is trying to kill her. She seeks refuge with her sister who is just days away from getting married. What happens?

489. Your hero is trying to save his family business by buying a competitor. Your heroine is determined not to sell. And someone is sabotaging them both while making it look like they're out to get each other. Once they figure it out, they must band together to find out who is fueling their feud.

490. Your heroine is nicknamed the "Beauty Queen Assassin." Why? What earned her the nickname? Start your story with the incident that earned her the nickname.

491. Your heroine runs an elite spa and her workers are turning up dead. Why?

492. A tornado hit town and demolished it. Your hero and heroine are trapped under some rubble. How do they survive until they are rescued?

493. Your hero or heroine reclaims and refurbishes old furniture and resells it. They find an old table and discover something hidden inside of it. What do they find?

494. Your heroine finds a baby in the back seat of her car., before she can take the baby to the police station someone tries to kill her. Why and what does she do?

495. Your heroine is house sitting for a friend or relative. She's sitting on the couch watching television when she hears something. She's 100% certain she's not alone. Is she?

496. Your heroine is digging in the garden and finds....

497. Your hero and heroine are trapped in a warehouse. (You decide why they're trapped.) Your heroine picks up something off of the top of a box. Her partner questions how she's going to use the item. And she shows them by using it to escape. What does she pick up? How do they escape?

498. Your heroine is hiding in the bushes while she watches a group of people release animals in the zoo. Why is she hiding?

499. Your hero is driving down the road. He sees a woman walking alone. It's getting late and starting to rain. He pulls over to pick her up and it's someone he knows. Who is it and why is she walking along the road?

500. Your heroine has a choice; get into a car with a jerk – someone she just can't stand, or stay and fight. What does she decide to do?

501. Your heroine is the leader of an elite group (you decide exactly who they work for and what they do). The problem is she's getting tired of risking her life for people who don't deserve it. After a particularly trying job she…. What does she do?

502. Your hero gets a call from his best friend. He's in trouble. What's happened?

503. Your heroine is a blogger. A frequent commenter is starting to get friendly – too friendly. It's starting to give her the creeps. What does she do?

504. Your heroine is at a bar trying to unwind after a terrible day. A bar fight breaks out. What does she do?

505. Your heroine learns an old family secret that changes her life. What does she learn and how does she find out?

506. Your heroine is investigating a murder and the only piece of evidence she has belongs to her. What is it and how is it connected to the murder?

507. Your heroine is on a trip. She's rented an ATV and is riding it with a group of people into the jungle. She flips her ATV, but no one notices. She rolls down a hill and lands in a muddy, bloody, lump at the bottom. She's hurt, but she's okay. After a while she starts climbing back up the hill, certain she's going in the right direction. What happens next?

508. Your hero/heroine has a new identity and a new life. They've just encountered someone who thinks they look familiar. What do they do?

509. Your heroine is a veterinarian. She arrives at her office one morning to find a large box with air holes. What's inside the box and what does she do with it?

510. After mourning his dead girlfriend, your hero receives a note telling him to meet her at a secret location. What's going on?

511. Your heroine is in handcuffs...how'd she get there? How does she get out of them?

512. Your heroine is at a costume party and someone is wearing the same costume she is. Someone tries to kill her at the party. Is it a case of mistaken identity or is someone out to get her?

513. Your hero or heroine is a teacher. When one of their students goes missing, they may have been the last person to see them. What happens?

514. Someone in your heroine's life envies her, so much so that they begin sabotaging her life and taking it over. What happens?

515. Your hero and his friend are competing in a dare. What's the dare? Who wins? What happens?

516. Your heroine loses a parking spot to a jerk. She starts to confront him, then gets creeped out and backs off. What creeps her out? What happens?

517. Your heroine is walking her dog in the woods when a bear crosses their path. What does she do?

518. Your heroine notices someone following a little girl in their pickup truck. When a man jumps out of his to grab the girl, your heroine…What does she do?

519. Your hero/heroine is getting a professional massage. The other is giving a massage. (For example, your heroine is getting the massage and your hero is giving it). The lights are dim.

Background music is playing. The room smells like essential oils. Everyone is relaxed. Shots ring out. People scream. What happens to your hero and heroine?

520. Your hero has rented a house from a friend. He gets off of the bus, walks to the address he's been given only to find a hot pink house with purple flower boxes waiting for him.

He can't "lie low" in a hot pink house. He calls his friend who is conveniently busy. His friend sends over his sister. Describe their interaction and the hero's first glimpse of the pink house.

521. Your heroine returns home to a small town to help a high school friend, now sheriff, with his police force. She's immediately entrenched in local politics and quickly makes some enemies. Now a powerful family wants her gone and they're not afraid to threaten her or her new boyfriend, a local journalist. What happens?

522. Your hero is camping when he finds a woman crying alone on the beach. She's suffered a great tragedy and it seems to have caused her to forget who she is and where she's from. What happens?

523. Your heroine is a mob boss's daughter. That means she's heavily guarded and always under scrutiny. Under an assumed name, she takes off to a remote cabin to get some peace.

After being rescued from an encounter with a bear, she develops a friendship with her rescuer and neighbor. Her father, who always has someone nearby watching her, learns of her new friend, investigates him and learns that he's an informer in the witness protection program.

His testimony put away a close friend/family member. Now he's gunning for your hero and your heroine is smack dab in the middle of it. What happens?

524. Someone is killing female radio personalities. On the advice of a friend your heroine (a radio personality) has hired her friend's brother to protect her. What happens?

525. Your hero is ex-military and a security expert. He'd just arrived at a friend's party only to find that the place has been bombed and most everyone is dead. After interviewing a few survivors, including a beautiful computer expert, he believes that the bombing is related to….

526. Your heroine is a tough assistant district attorney. She never pleads out a case. Now she's up against the hot attorney representing a man she despises, a man accused of killing his wife. What happens when they get face to face?

527. Your heroine is a pharmacist. On her way to her car after the store has closed, she is held at gunpoint by a man who wants drugs. Who saves her? How?

528. Your heroine is on volunteer highway cleanup. Her organization sponsors a portion of the local highway and

once every couple of months they head out, put on their orange vests, and clean up the garbage. Today she finds something unusual. What does she find? What are the repercussions of her discovery?

529. Your heroine's ex-husband's mistress is found murdered and the gun that killed her is found in your heroine's car. She's being framed, of course. Start your story when she learns that her ex's mistress is dead.

530. Your heroine has a mysterious virus. The doctors that are researching a cure are killed and your heroine is being followed. Why?

531. Your hero wakes up in jail and doesn't know how he got there. The only clue is a piece of paper he finds in his pocket. What does it say?

532. Your heroine is alone on vacation, or so she thinks. Who is watching her and why?

533. Your heroine is sneaking away from her controlling husband at night to help people in her community. Her husband hires a man to follow her. When he finds out what she's doing does he turn her in?

534. Your heroine passes out on the street. She's rushed to the hospital by a Good Samaritan. When she wakes, she learns she's been injected with the virus. The only way to find a cure is to find the person who injected her. What happens?

535. Your heroine receives a mysterious message from her past. It's warning her that a killer is after her. What does she do?

536. Your hero and heroine are after the same man. One is an investigator and the other is after him for personal reasons. When your investigator sets a trap for him the other shows up just in time to complicate matters. Who are they after and why?

537. Your heroine's son or daughter witnessed a crime and now the criminals are after them. What lengths will your heroine go to protect her child?

538. Your heroine is leaving the hospital when she's kidnapped. She's mistaken as a nurse. Her kidnapper is on the run and needs medical attention. Why is he on the run and what does he do when he learns his "nurse" isn't really equipped to help him.

539. Your heroine is sure her younger sister, a journalist, stumbled onto a human trafficking ring and has been captured. Your heroine starts digging and meets your hero. Where does she meet him and how does he get involved?

540. Your hero shows up at work only to find that his boss has been murdered. The police arrest him for the crime. He's being framed and only the quiet cop with the deep brown eyes seems to believe he's innocent. How do they clear his name?

541. Your heroine feels like someone is following her. She hires a personal investigator to see who it is. What happens?

542. Your hero met a girl down by the river one day. They played all day long, catching frogs and swinging on a rope swing over the river. The next day all anyone could talk about was a missing girl – his new friend had disappeared. Now he's working alongside a woman that triggers

memories of that day by the river. Who is she? What happened to that girl?

543. Your heroine discovers that her husband is running a ponzi scheme; he's stealing money from her friends and family. She turns to the son of a family friend, and stock market analyst, to help her prove her husband is stealing. Before they can gather enough proof he's onto them, and he has hired someone to kill them. What happens?

544. A woman shows up at his Costa Rican surfing resort applying for a job and your hero is sure she's hiding something. A day after he hires her, killers are gunning for her and your hero feels compelled to keep her safe. Who is she? Why are killers after her? What happens?

545. Your heroine is finally living out her dream of starting a lavender farm. Out in the field she finds a body with a message attached to it. The body was left for her to find. More bodies show up, each with a new message for her. Can the new sheriff in town help her before she's added to the body count?

546. Your heroine is in the witness protection program and someone has found her. It's up to your hero to keep her safe and hide her while the threat is eliminated. What happens? Why is she in the witness protection program?

547. Your hero and heroine are trapped on the roof of a skyscraper. Why? What happens?

548. Your heroine is convinced that her neighbor is a dirty cop. She sees him meeting with all sorts of "undesirables." She decides to do a little investigating herself and ends up getting into heaps of trouble. Her neighbor bails her out, but not before he teaches her a lesson or two about

snooping. What does she learn and how does he bail her out?

549. Your heroine's sister is convicted of killing her husband – a politician and a world class jerk – but your heroine is convinced she didn't do it. Can she prove her sister's innocence before she's sent to prison for the rest of her life? What happens when she stumbles on the truth?

550. Your hero's military commander had one dying wish, for your hero to protect his daughter. Your hero isn't sure why she needs protection, but he'd do anything for the leader that saved his life. Why does she need protecting and what happens when your hero first meets your heroine?

Notes:

_____

_____

_____

_____

_____

_____

_____

_____

_____

_____

_____

_____

_____

_____

_____

_____

_____

Chapter 5

Western, Inspirational

551. Your heroine is on the run from a bad boyfriend. She gets a job at a ranch out West and makes her way there, hoping to hide out and maybe make a new life for herself.

owner of the ranch, a dark and brooding man, is secretive and angry. There's a strong attraction between them. What happens when her ex finds her? Why is the rancher secretive and angry?

552. Your heroine is sorting through her grandma's belongings in an attic. She finds a large pink hatbox. She opens it. What does she find?

553. Your hero walks into the garage. He's passing through this small town, he's a city guy, and his car breaks down. He meets your heroine, the garage owner and a mechanic, and doesn't know what to do with the fact that she's both beautiful and obviously more skilled with a wrench than he is. How does he react? What happens?

554. There's a beautiful, somewhat melancholy song by Neko Case called, "I Wish I Was the Moon." Here are some of the lyrics:

"How will you know if you found me at last?

'Cause I'll be the one, be the one, be the one

With my heart in my lap

I'm so tired, I'm so tired

And I wish I was the moon tonight."

Perhaps start your story from your hero's perspective. What has happened to him to bring him to this lonely place? What choices has he made that have resulted in weariness and loneliness? Now, whom does he meet that brings the sunshine back into his life and how does she do it?

555. Your heroine is living a life that just doesn't fit her. She's a country girl living in the big city and struggling to feel at home. On a whim she takes a road trip out West to revisit her roots and discovers...What, or who, does she discover? How does it/he change her life and her perspective?

556. Your heroine gave up her dreams, instead marrying and becoming the wife of a rancher. She never expected the marriage to end in tragedy, leaving her a widow and the unwelcome owner of a huge ranch.

When a company offers her millions for her ranch, she must decide if she's ready to say goodbye to her husband's dreams and start living her own again.

This could be the beginning of a wonderful contemporary romance. It also sets the stage for a good western romance – imagine the community rallying around her to help her keep the ranch and a hunky ranch hand who helps her realize her future is here on the land that she inherited.

Or the sexy lawyer who helps her negotiate a deal that is a win/win for the entire town and helps fulfill her husband's dying wishes.

There's also plenty of room for suspense. Water rights, oil rights, and valuable land are all great motives for foul play!

557. Your heroine is a veritable Santa's Little Helper. She's working hard at her local community center to help bring the holiday spirit to families in need. She meets a little girl who is in desperate need for some Christmas hope and cheer.

Your heroine makes her way to the little girl's home to bring her a few holiday decorations and meets the girl's dad. Describe the interaction and their first meeting. Why does the little girl need holiday hope and how does your heroine provide it?

558. Your heroine witnesses a group of football fans on their way to a big game stop and assist and old lady. She catches the eye of one of the Good Samaritans and smiles. He smiles back. What happens next?

559. A wealthy woman works hard to keep her family's foundation to end homelessness running smoothly, though at times she feels her efforts are for naught. A routine visit to the local homeless shelter changes her life when she meets a man. Who is he and how does he change her life?

560. Your heroine just won the lottery and she has no idea what on earth to do with her winnings. Sure enough, though, people are coming out of the woodwork to tell her how to manage it.

In a fit of despair, she takes off to a new town where she meets someone who changes her life. Where does she go? Who does she meet and how do they change her life?

561. Serving her community service sentence, your heroine is volunteering. While volunteering she meets a fellow comrade also sentenced to community service. What did

they each do to earn community service, where are they working and what happens when they meet?

562. Your mild mannered heroine is having a horrible day. On her walk home, because her car won't start, she comes across a man who is harassing a woman.

Fed up with the way people treat each other, she steps in to help and ends up in the hospital. Though maybe her day is looking up when a handsome police office comes in to take her statement, and her phone number. What happened to put her in the hospital and what happens with the handsome police officer?

563. On vacation, your hero or heroine is sentenced to community service for a small crime (for example, accidentally stealing chips from a small town gas station). This community service forces him or her to stay in this small town to serve their time. Who do they meet and what happens to change their life?

564. Your heroine is determined to get her dad's failing ranch back in the black, but her new trainer has a different way of doing things. In short, they, t heads. Why don't they get along? What happens that helps them come together?

565. Your heroine left the Amish world and vowed she'd never go back. Now her sister's mysterious death is calling her home. Back amongst the people she left behind, she meets a newcomer.

He's handsome and mysterious. Yet all signs point to him being the killer. Can she trust him with her life and her heart, or is he the killer?

566. Your heroine just inherited her sister's toddler. Her sister just took off and left her kid. Your heroine has no desire to have a kid, and no time in her busy life to raise one, but she feels a sense of responsibility for the boy and wants to do the right thing. A handyman working on renovations in her home forges an instant connection with the little boy and helps your heroine in more ways than she ever imagined.

567. The way to a man's heart is through his stomach, right? So why does the owner of the best deli in town have such a hard time with men?

568. Your heroine owns a Texas-sized ranch in Oklahoma. When a local hot shot moves in and buys the land surrounding hers the trouble starts. He wants her land. She's not going to part with it.

Rich men don't know anything about ranching; they kill the land and turn it into nothing but dust. She chooses to take the high road and ignore the guy.

But when her river suddenly dries up she can't take anymore. She confronts him face to face. Unfortunately all of her assumptions are wrong. Why is her water drying up and how does she come to grips with the fact that her worst enemy isn't as bad as he seems. In fact, he may be her soul mate?

569. Your heroine is a bit of an observer. Well that's what she calls herself. Others would call her a voyeur. She even peeps through windows from time to time. She has a kind heart and turns her "peeping" into good deeds.

When she observes a man doing something surprising she surprises herself with her reaction. What does she observe him do? Who is he? What does she do?

570. A soap opera star is fired. Actually, her show is canceled. Having been on the soap since she was a child she's not sure she's qualified to do anything else. She has a very public reaction and is now the fodder for tabloids everywhere. Needing to hide she heads to a small town. Who does she meet and how does she come to grips with her new life?

571. Your heroine is caring for a loved one during their final days. The loved one, maybe it's a beloved grandmother, asks your character to help her resolve something before she dies. It's something she regrets.

What does the dying relative ask your heroine to do and who does she meet?

572. "What have I done with my life?" Your hero or heroine is facing this dilemma. They're about to go into battle or otherwise put themselves in danger. You decide who is putting themselves in danger and why. Maybe your hero is going to rescue his girlfriend's daughter from the mob or from bad ranchers.

573. It's Thanksgiving and your heroine goes for a walk to escape family drama. Halfway across town your hero does the same thing. How do they meet?

574. Your heroine is standing on an empty street. The wind is whipping and her long coat is open and flapping behind her. She arches her back, spreads her arms out wide and embraces the chill. Why?

575. Your heroine is in the jungle searching for a plant that may be the next medical miracle. She stumbles upon drug dealers and before she can get away unnoticed, she is captured. Who captures her and what happens next?

576. Your heroine has landed a job as an extra on a film. She attends a crazy party with the leading man and wakes up naked next to a dead man. She doesn't remember a thing and suspicion is pointed at her. What happened? How does she prove her innocence? Is she innocent?

577. A woman writing a book at a street corner cafe notices a man following a woman. It looks suspicious to her so she quickly gathers her things and follows him. What does she see? Who is he and why is he following that woman?

578. What is one thing you've always wanted to do? Sky dive? Rock climb? Go scuba diving? Hire a professional shopper? Your heroine is ticking off her bucket list and she's starting with the biggest item on her list. What is it? What happens when she checks it off her list?

579. Your heroine runs a garage, she's a mechanic. She lives in the South where racing is a big deal and gender roles sometimes feel as if they're back in the 1800s. When a hot shot racer from out of town needs his car fixed, he's surprised to find a woman mechanic. What happens when he sees your hot heroine under the hood of his car?

580. Your heroine is five minutes from giving a presentation. She is dreading it. Someone says something to her that either makes it worse or makes it better. Who are they? What do they say?

581. Your hero is a dance teacher and is accustomed to his students crushing on him. But he's not prepared for his

feelings for one new student. What happens? What makes this new student special?

582. Your heroine discovers her fiancée has been cheating by seeing him on the cover of a tabloid magazine. What does she do?

583. Your heroine is a Dr. Doolittle. She picks up stray animals, which seem to come her way on a regular basis, and she cares for them. One of the animals she's been caring for has an owner. What happens when they first meet?

584. Your hero is visiting someone in the hospital when he meets a woman who is visiting the same person. They've never met each other before. Who are they visiting and what happens next?

585. Your hero is tracking a wayward wife. When she leads him to a club, he's tempted to join in. What kind of club did she lead him to and what is the conflict for your hero? Why is he hesitant to join in?

586. Your heroine just learned that she has a sister. How does she learn? What does she do next?

587. Your hero left home when he was a teenager. Now, scary dreams and changes to his body have sent him home for answers. What's happening and what does he find when he gets home?

588. Your hero was tricked into joining a matchmaking service. He's unhappy about it until he meets the owner of the service. She's the one he wants, but she has a strict rule, she never dates clients. How does he change her mind?

589. Fracking is destroying your heroine's ranch and she's afraid for the health of her community. Not one to let big business push her around she takes her battle right to the front door of the owner of the gas company. What happens?

590. Your heroine is a new nurse at a prominent hospital. When a terminal patient is found dead she suspects his doctor assisted in the patient's suicide. She must decide for herself how she feels about the doctor and about assisted suicide.

591. Your heroine is doing mission work for her church. When she falls for a fellow missionary she begins to question her beliefs. Why?

592. Your hero learns that his wife's death wasn't an accident. What happened?

593. Your heroine's grandparents just died in a forest fire and it's up to her to manage their estate and clean up. What she finds when she arrives at the small suffering town in Colorado surprises her.

594. Your hero is at a dude ranch. It's a family reunion and he's not really having a great time with his family. He heads out on his own one day and meets someone. Who does he meet?

595. He met her a decade ago at summer camp. He never forgot her. His job has brought him back to that summer town. He's taken the opportunity to walk around the abandoned camp. He walks up to his old cabin and the door opens. Who is standing there?

596. Your heroine inherits an abandoned ski resort. A local global resort wants to buy the property from her, but it was her dying grandfather's wish that she see the resort back to its former glory. Your heroine must recruit help and rally her community to help her. What does she do?

597. Inspired to volunteer at the local food share, your heroine meets a homeless person who changes her life. What happens?

598. Your heroine is fulfilling a bucket list wish and she's sleeping at the top of a lighthouse. What happens?

599. Your heroine is working for one of the most prestigious labs in the world. She stumbles upon a secret project – a potentially immoral project. What happens next?

600. Your hero is sitting at the wedding of the woman he loves. What does he do?

601. Your heroine just received bad news at the doctor. On her way out the door she slams into someone. He can tell she's been crying. What does he do or say?

602. Your heroine has a gun in her hand and she's aiming it at....

603. Your heroine receives a quilt made by the women in her family. It has been handed down from generation to generation along with another tradition – your heroine isn't interested in passing on the traditions.

What is the other tradition that's coupled with the quilt, and why isn't your heroine interested in participating? What happens?

604. Your heroine doesn't know who her father is and her mother just died, not telling her. She decides to connect with her mother's old friends to find out the answer to her question. Who does she meet and what does she learn?

605. Your hero is searching for his son. His girlfriend left him and disappeared when she was pregnant. He's on the hunt for his son and finds him in the last place he expects. How does he learn he has a son? Where does he find him?

606. Your heroine's fiancé died suddenly. She moves in with her brother and his wife. They convince her to go to the town festival and arrange a blind date. Is it too much too soon or is she ready for love?

607. Your heroine has attracted the attention of her father's fiercest rival. He plans to seduce her and use her for vengeance and leverage. He doesn't expect to fall in love. What happens?

608. Your hero is out to catch a bank robber. He tracks him down to his mistress's house, but his bank robber isn't there. He decides to wait and rents a room in her apartment building.

Day after day he gets to know her better and begins to lose focus on his goal of catching the bank robber. What does he do when he learns she's not the robber's mistress…she's his sister? What does she do when she learns her new friend is using her to capture her brother?

609. Your heroine is sneaking out of a building. She falls and is fortunately caught, by a handsome cowboy. Why is she sneaking out of the building and what does she do with her new friend?

610. Your heroine is on the run from her ex-lover. She needs his old partner to help her, but he's just been thrown in jail. She conjures up a ruse to get him out of jail and winds up getting herself in over her head. What does she do and why is she on the run from her ex-lover?

611. Your heroine is a preschool teacher. Moving from Boston, she gets a new job in rural Montana and receives an initial bad impression of the Big Sky State. A handsome firefighter helps her change her opinion and convinces her to stay. What happens to give her the initial bad impression?

612. Her mother's failing health brings your heroine back to her home town where she immediately comes face to face with her ex. He left her for the rodeo and never looked back. Now he's determined to get her back. What happens?

613. Your hero and heroine start your story on their wedding day. Before they can head off to their honeymoon, one of them disappears. What happens?

614. Your heroine is an aspiring country western singer on her way to Nashville to be discovered. Her car breaks down in the middle of nowhere and she's forced to take a part time waitressing gig to pay for her car's repairs. What happens to make your heroine question her path to fame and fortune and consider staying in the small town?

615. Your heroine is on an adventure and searching for a cowboy to make her girlfriends jealous. She doesn't plan on falling in love, just having a little fun. But when she meets your hero, her plans change. Why? What happens?

616. Your hero has a weak spot for a girl in red boots. When your heroine blows into town she's wearing the

sexiest pair of red boots he's ever seen. He's determined to get her out of her boots, but she's possibly more trouble than she's worth. What happens?

617. Your heroine owns and operates a holiday sleigh ride business in Colorado. She hitches a sleigh to her team of horses and takes tourists into the mountains on a romantic ride. When a snow storm catches her off guard she leads her customers to a small ranch owned by your hero. What happens?

618. Your heroine moves to a small town in Colorado to be close to her boyfriend, who promptly dumps her. Her first day on her new job as a bank teller and the bank is robbed. Just when she thinks it can't get any worse she meets your hero. What happens? Who is he? How do they meet?

619. Your heroine just bought a dilapidated ranch and thinks she's doing just fine repairing it until the sheriff tells her that he thinks she has a dangerous outlaw hiding on her property. When her horses escape and her barn burns down he just might be right. What happens?

620. When her boyfriend makes a very public debacle of himself and marries the new fiery redhead in town only days after she catches them together, your heroine is determined to get even with him.

She sets her sights on the new doctor in town. After all, the best revenge is living well, right? Might as well live well on the arm of the handsome, and rich, doctor. However, all the single women in town have their sights set on him too. How does your heroine try to capture his attention? What happens?

621. Your heroine's friends have decided she's the perfect match for their new minister. She admits that he's attractive, but resists her friends' encouragement. This forces them to get creative. What do they do to get your heroine and hero together?

622. Your heroine is extremely sentimental. Her mother died when she was young and she keeps a trunk full of memories in her home. When her home catches fire she's willing to risk her life to save the trunk.

A fireman rescues her and the trunk, but his bravery costs him. He loses his legs and his spirit to live. It's up to your heroine to prove to him that his life is worth living. How does she do it?

623. Your heroine is a bitter heiress. All she's ever known is betrayal and deception. She's certainly never trusted any man. Can your hero, an architect working on remodeling her home, teach her about faith and trust?

624. Your heroine, on her way home for the holidays, misses her train. Now she's stranded. Not that she cares much about missing her family's holiday celebration. She doesn't get along with them and the holidays don't mean anything to her anymore.

She does care that the train station is closing and she has nowhere to go. That is, until the owner of the café invites her to stay with him. What does he do to teach her the true meaning of Christmas?

625. Your hero's wife died seven years ago and he's still not over it. On what would have been their anniversary he drinks too much, sees a vision of his dead wife, and follows her. It's not his dead wife, but a woman who is very much

alive. Who is she? What does she do with the drunken man that's following her?

626. Your heroine just opened up a kite store in a small harbor town. The first day she's open, a small child comes in with their dad. It's clear the young girl is autistic and it's clear that the dad isn't sure what to do with his daughter.

The young girl finds the kites to be fascinating and seems to make a connection with your heroine who understands autism all too well. What happens?

627. Your heroine's husband is missing in action. Every night she prays for his return. What happens?

628. The church's annual festival is coming up and your hero and heroine are right in the middle of the planning action. However, your hero doesn't know that right after the festival, your heroine is leaving town. Why? What does he do when he finds out?

629. Your heroine is a motivational speaker. When one of her fans gets a little to crazed she is forced to hire a bodyguard. The fan tests her faith and the bodyguard tests promises she made to herself. What happens? Does she pass her own tests?

630. Your heroine's on her way to a gospel festival. She's competitive and proud of her gospel choir. However, she's definitely not prepared for the other choirs or the leader of their rival choir. What happens when she meets him?

631. Your heroine is determined to get a famous country singer to sing for her brother's orphanage fund raiser. Without a lot of cash, the orphanage will close. What does

she do to convince the country singer to devote his talents to her cause?

632. After a terrible scandal in your heroine's hospital she heads to Africa to work in a Doctors Without Borders facility. What she finds there changes her life forever. What happens?

633. Your heroine is molested by her priest as a child. As an adult she's struggling with her beliefs. How does a new co-worker change her opinion of religion and god?

634. Your hero's faith is important to him. What does he do when he falls for a woman who doesn't believe in the same God he does? How do they meet and fall in love?

635. Your heroine prays every day that God will help her move past the death of her husband and child. When a new renter moves into her basement apartment has God finally answered her prayers? What happens? How does your heroine let go of her past and move forward?

636. Your heroine owns a voodoo shop in New Orleans She doesn't believe in it, but the tourists flock to her store and keep her in business. She's disenchanted with society and believes the worst in people. One day a man walks in and with one simple action, he changes her mind. How? What does he say or do?

637. Your heroine, an FBI agent, is sent to an Amish community to protect a citizen. Why? Who does she meet when she's there and what does she learn?

638. Your heroine moves her family to rural Pennsylvania and meets an Amish man who may change her life and the life of her young children. What does he do? How does he

overcome his community's distrust of outsiders to help your heroine and her family?

639. When a pregnant woman shows up at his doorstep, the new homeowner isn't sure what else to do. He invites her inside. She gives birth in his home moments later. How does your hero reconcile his growing feelings for this mysterious, and unmarried, woman with his faith and upbringing?

640. Your heroine is being held hostage by a bunch of outlaws that are using her farm home as a hideaway. When her handsome neighbor comes calling she tries to get him to leave, but he is suspicious. What happens?

641. Your heroine is able to talk to people who have passed away. When a grief stricken woman comes to her for help, she gets grief from the woman's son. Sparks fly and she feels compelled to help both the mother and her adult son come to grips with the death of their beloved family member and find hope again.

642. Your heroine gets a visit from an angel. Why? What happens when she sees the angel for the first time?

643. Your hero has a dream that prompts him to head into the jungle. What did he dream about and what does he discover in the jungle?

644. Your heroine travels to Israel to learn about her heritage. When she's there she meets the son of her father's first love. As they grow close they discover that they might be siblings. What happens?

645. Your hero makes hand crafted Western styled furniture. He lives alone on a large ranch and likes it that

way. He prefers his solitude. What does he do when a famous designer tries to convince him to take his hand crafted furniture mainstream? And what does she learn about living a quieter life in rural Montana?

646. Your heroine witnesses a drive by shooting. The trauma triggers memories of a traumatic event from her past. She seeks psychiatric help and meets an angel in the mental hospital. What happens? Is he really an angel or has she completely lost her mind?

647. Your heroine works for her dad as a blacksmith in the Wild West. A man walks into her shop one day and asks her to make a special item. What does he request and why?

648. Your heroine is an author who writes spicy stories under a penname. What happens when the people of her quiet Amish community learn that she's the author?

649. Your heroine is in a car accident and sees her dead best friend beside her while she's unconscious. She wakes in the hospital and is delighted to learn that her guardian angel is still beside her.

Why is he there? What is his mission? How does she react when she learns why he's been sent?

650. Everything your heroine ever thought she knew about herself and her family has been turned upside down. She'll need the support of her friends and a few strangers to help her get through the surprise. What does she learn about herself and her family and how does your hero help her?

Notes:

Chapter 6

In Their Own Words

Start your story with....

651. "My, my, my. The apple doesn't fall far from the tree..."

652. "My aim is usually better..."

653. "Two frogs walk into a bar."

654. "I'm sorry, I don't speak Russian."

655. "Of all the wicked little..."

656. "You're afraid I am going to die tonight?"

657. "You have the morals of a chimpanzee."

658. "Well sure, everyone is entitled to their own opinion. It's just that yours is stupid."

659. "Do you remember the time we..?"

660. "I'm feeling kind of orange today."

661. "What the hell am I supposed to do with this?"

662. "If you answer, I won't hurt you more."

663. "I like you better when you're not talking."

664. "Too bad, you might have lived to see the new age."

665. "I'm not the girl your mother warned you about. Her imagination was never this good."

666. "Then don't eat the damned sandwich."

667. "With this ring, I thee wed."

668. "So, you gonna sleep with him or not?"

669. "I can't believe I…."

670. "You'd better go in disguise."

671. "They've just taken her hostage."

672. "I haven't seen you for more than a hundred years, literally."

673. "It's just a harmless little lie."

674. "I'm changing my name to…."

675. "Oh no, not you again."

676. "I have nothing left to lose."

677. "Read 'em and weep."

678. "Why don't you come a little closer?"

679. "I need to learn how to pleasure a man."

680. "Ah, shit. She's a princess? A real life princess?"

681. "Mmm, hmmm, sweet as sin."

682. "I'm so tired I could sleep on an airport floor."

683. "You might want to go a little lighter with the body spray?"

684. "I just want you to be happy."

685. "Did you know I used to raise chickens?"

686. "You're not trying hard enough."

"I'm trying as hard as I can."

687. "I wouldn't get into a car with you if my life were on the line."

688. "Didn't your mother ever tell you not to play with fire?"

689. "It's not like the garden gnomes are speaking to you, right?"

690. "I've only hit a person once and he deserved it. Don't make me do it again."

691. "Looks like your jigsaw puzzle is missing a few pieces. Who'd you pick a fight with this time?"

692. "Why are you in my head again?"

693. Speaker One: "Aren't you going to do anything about him?"

Speaker Two: "No, the world is full of bigger creeps than him."

694. "Where'd you learn to do that?"

695. "Your standards are too high."

"Why, because he has to be smart, kind, nice to look at, great in bed, and able to juggle?"

696. "I think you're sitting on…."

697. "What the heck kind of bird is that?"

"I don't think that's a bird."

698. "I'm sorry, officer I …"

699. "If he is a fireman someone pleeease light me on fire. Whoo."

700. "Oh, I could just kiss him. If only he…."

701. "Some people just don't know when to leave well enough alone."

702. "I think something's on fire…"

703. "I lied on my resume."

704. "What did you wish for?"

705. "Are you still pissed at me?"

706. "That is the freakiest cat…"

707. "Well, what do you think?"

708. "I'm so tired I could cry."

"You want to have sex?"

709. "I'm far from the child you remember."

710. "You're wearing that?"

711. "I heard that she earned her fortune by…"

712. "I think you've had too much to drink."

713. "No, I don't wanna wake up. Not yet."

714. "This is private property, you're trespassing on. My private property."

715. "Is that your dog?"

716. "Someone's been sleeping in my bed and they're still there."

717. "Drive it like you stole it."

718. "They're both perfect on paper. I'm dating two great guys and I don't want either of them. What's wrong with me?"

719. "You're daring me to…? You should know better."

720. "You don't see her for who she is."

721. "I guess I have to face the facts. Someone really is trying to kill me."

722. "Going to church doesn't make you a Christian any more than standing in a garage makes you a car."

723. "I once prayed to God for a bike, but quickly found out he didn't work that way…so I stole a bike and prayed for his forgiveness."

724. "Expecting the world to treat you fairly because you are good is like expecting the bull not to charge because you are a vegetarian."

725. "It may look like I'm doing nothing, but I'm actively waiting for my problems to go away."

726. "Men marry because they are tired, women because they are curious; both are disappointed."

727. "It's not polite to bite your neighbors."

728. "I promise it won't hurt…much."

729. "That's the most beautiful____ I've ever seen."

730. "Anyone who says he can see through women is missing a lot." – Groucho Marx

731. "Between two evils I always pick the one I've never tried before." – Mae West

732. "Happiness is having a large loving close knit family in another city." – George Burns

733. "I feel sorry for the people who don't drink. When they wake up in the morning that's as good as they're going to feel all day." – Frank Sinatra

734. "I'm an idealist. I don't know where I am going, but I am on my way." – Carl Sandberg

735. "If love is the answer, could you please rephrase the question?" – Lily Tomlin

736. "If two wrongs don't make a right, try three." – Laurence J. Peter

737. "Give a man a match, and he'll be warm for a minute, but set him on fire, and he'll be warm for the rest of his life."

738. "I faked it. Every single time."

739. "I never learned to count my blessings. I choose to dwell on my disasters instead." – Ray LaMontagne

740. "I've been to hell and back so many times you kinda bore me." – Ray LaMontagne

741. "Men love harder than women. They're more passionate."

"You've been lovin' the wrong women."

742. "Someone's gonna pay for this."

743. "What we've got here is failure to communicate."

744. "Wasn't it Norman Bates that said a boy's best friend is his mother?"

"You think he might be creepy?"

"Don't you?"

745. "Joy to the world and all that crap."

746. "She looks like she ate…"

"A canary?"

"No, a whole darned peacock."

747. "Well, sugar, aren't you just a bottomless pit of joy and inspiration?"

748. "I think you just knocked my tooth loose."

749. "I just shot him. Should I apologize or shoot him again?"

750. "I'm melting like, butter in the hot sun."

Notes:

_____
_____
_____
_____
_____
_____
_____
_____
_____
_____
_____
_____
_____
_____
_____
_____
_____
_____
_____
_____
_____
_____
_____
_____
_____
_____
_____

Chapter 7

Set the Scene

Start your story with…

751. The door burst open.

752. The voice inside her head giggled with sadistic glee.

753. She knelt at the altar and hoped it wasn't too late.

754. They say that life shrinks or expands in proportion to one's courage.

755. Eclipses always make me twitchy.

756. Under the full sun, he bared his fangs. A low growl, seemingly unheard by those that stood nearby on the sidewalk, emanated from his throat.

757. She/I couldn't help, but stare at…

758. She dipped her…

759. I'd like you to meet your future husband; your betrothed.

760. Today I follow my heart and discover my destiny.

761. He was a chiropractor. How dangerous could he be?

762. You can sleep here for the night. The boss won't be back until tomorrow.

763. That was the moment her heart stopped beating.

764. She heard him before she saw him. His rich voice massaged her senses and sent waves of pleasure over her body.

765. The average woman would rather have beauty than brains, because the average man can see better than he can think.

766. Taking one step down the stairs, she gripped the hammer and listened.

767. The loud boom shook her home and brought tears to her eyes.

768. The dead bird lying at her feet had to be a bad omen.

769. There's a fine line between pain and pleasure.

770. She gasped, surprised to feel such delicious joy.

771. His torso rippled with lean muscle. A jagged scar stretched over his ribs.

772. I knew I was making a big mistake, but still I held out my hand and we shook on it.

773. I felt like a metal ball in one of those old pinball machines.

774. She looked down at her red shoes and prayed a house would fall on her.

775. I was grinning so hard my face hurt.

776. He hit the ground like a sack of flour. She shook her hand, certain she'd broken a few bones.

777. Being dead sucks.

778. His motto of live fast, die young and leave a good looking corpse caught up to him – much sooner than he'd expected.

779. He was not afraid of her – a woman who equaled his will and strength.

780. He/she had given up on redemption.

781. She allowed herself to be mesmerized by his…

782. People are like slinkies, not really good for much of anything except brining a smile to your face when you push them down the stairs.

783. One more step and I'll be an outlaw. Hunted by everyone with an ax to grind or a buck to earn.

784. Jane Austen made me do it.

785. I really should have known better.

786. It's hard to love an assassin.

787. Never trust an angel.

788. She swung the crowbar over her head as a warning. He didn't heed it.

789. He'd experienced 82 ways to die.

790. I peered out the windshield of my….

791. Someone was in my home. In my wildest dreams it would be…

792. What would she do when she saw him? Maybe a better question would be what would he do when they came face to face?

793. She hung up the phone. Nothing would ever be the same again.

794. She wanted him almost more than she wanted her next breath.

795. She clenched her fists at her side, determined not to punch the jerk in the face. She knew the only solution was to walk away before she did something she regretted. She turned. He grabbed her hand.

796. I sat high above him in the tree and watched.

797. He leaned in close to her and whispered, "Destiny is not a matter of chance. It is a matter of choice."

798. It's never too late to become the person you want to be.

799. Victory belongs to….

800. She looked at him and without hesitation said, "Success is a state of mind."

801. She squinted in the bright sunlight. Sweat trickled down her spine. Standing, she put her hands on her hips. "What's your story?" she said.

802. He knew she wouldn't be happy to see him.

803. As much as she irritated him, he enjoyed seeing the challenge in her eyes.

804. How can you forgive when you can never forget?

805. Some sins are worth dying for.

806. Priorities, she thought. Shelter, heat, food.

807. She smelled like lemon meringue pie.

808. He could tell she was a woman. No man ever moved like that. So why was she disguised as a man? She wasn't fooling anyone. Okay, maybe she was. Judging from the hearty slap on the back she just received, some people bought her act. But she certainly wasn't fooling him.

809. She held tight to the steering wheel, willing the car to make the tight corner. The right wheels left the pavement. "Come on," she said, urging it to stay upright.

810. Judging from the look on his face, she hadn't made her intended impression.

811. The snow floated through the lattice of branches overhead.

812. She'd lost all feeling in the tip of her nose. Her fingers were painfully numb and she realized she couldn't feel her feet. It was time to find shelter, fast.

813. Without the hum of the motor, the silence in the air was both peaceful and terrifying. He couldn't dwell on it. He had to find a place to land.

814. Her big Disney princess eyes looked at him in surprise.

815. She looked in her rear view mirror and groaned. Looks like she had a tail again today. Her own personal stalker.

816. He shoved down the guilt and focused on his objective. He'd deal with the guilt later, and the regret.

817. She opened her eyes, blinked twice and struggled to focus. Nothing looked familiar.

818. The snoring woke her. Her dog must have climbed into her bed during the night. She rolled over. A small squeak escaped her lips. It wasn't her dog that was snoring. It was…

819. She looked up at his extended hand and ignored it. She'd gotten this far on her own. She didn't need his help getting up off her ass. She shoved to her feet and pushed past him.

820. The warm liquid burned her throat and soothed her soul.

821. Looking at the scoundrel she shook her head. She should have listened to her mother.

822. Everything hurt. Every muscle, and things she assumed were muscles, hurt. How did this happen?

823. She couldn't outrun the memories, but she could try.

824. If I knew how I'd gotten to this point, I'd know how to make changes. Trouble was, I had no idea how I'd gotten here. I couldn't remember.

825. She baked cupcakes for a living. He pictured her covered with frosting then shook the delicious image from his mind. He was here on business.

826. She heard the carolers from her couch and debated opening the door. The last thing she wanted was to see a crowd of cheerful faces.

827. She waved the paper in front of her face in a desperate attempt to cool down.

828. She dropped to the ground in exhaustion, unsure she'd ever be able to get up again.

829. The future of her people rested on my shoulders and at the present moment I could barely give a damn. They'd let me down, again.

830. I knew he was made for me the first time I saw him.

831. They were speaking, and she knew she should be paying attention, but she had other, more dire, thoughts on her mind.

832. He knew I was lying. I could tell by the way his right eyebrow rose up. Weird how he could do that, raise one eyebrow at a time. I couldn't let his facial quirks, as attractive as they were, derail me. I needed to convince him that I was telling the truth.

833. He walked away and I couldn't help but notice his, ass. Wowza, what a backside he had. The kind that looked so good in jeans you had to clench your fists to resist squeezing it.

834. The smell hit her first. It filled her throat, burned her eyes, and wove its way down inside her lungs.

835. She looked out at the crowd and her knees buckled. He was right behind her, ready to catch her fall.

836. I pulled my cloak tighter around me. The chill in the air battled with my will. I was afraid it was winning as I shivered and took another step in the knee deep snow.

837. A little voice whispered a warning. As usual, I ignored it. I would regret it later.

838. Lightening sliced the sky. The air crackled. It fueled him. He stretched out his arms and willed the clouds to open up.

839. Not bothering to hang up, she threw the phone across the room. It shattered in a glorious electronic explosion. She instantly regretted it. Now she'd have to buy a new phone.

840. He took off his hat and ran his fingers through his hair. It'd been a long day and it didn't look like it was going to end soon.

841. She stared at the body and willed herself to stay quiet. Tears threatened to spill from her eyes. She'd stay strong. She had to.

842. Her head throbbed painfully – as if a small child were ramming a toy car into it over and over again. She opened her eyes and glared at the small child.

843. She rolled her eyes for the fifth time during their conversation. This time she didn't care if he saw her or not.

844. It's not like he disliked the man standing in front of him. He just didn't trust him.

845. He saw the ring on her finger and felt the joy leave his body – as if someone had just kicked it out of him.

846. She had a decision to make. Turn to the enemy or go it alone. It should be an easy decision, but it was proving to be an impossible choice.

847. She held on for dear life and refused to look down.

848. She stepped into her shoes, grabbed her towel and sunglasses and prepared for a day of rest and relaxation.

849. Her head bobbed enthusiastically, like one of those dashboard bobbleheads, and I swear if she said "great" one more time I was going to laugh through my nose. Could someone really be this excited about work?

850. She took a bite and allowed the flavors to roll over her tongue. It was delicious, better than sex – or at least better than sex with her present company.

851. She saw him raise the sword and bring it down in a powerful thrust. Her heart stopped beating.

Notes:

_____

_____

_____

_____

_____

_____

_____

_____

_____

_____

_____

_____

Chapter 8

Erotic Romance

852. A man watches a woman through binoculars. Who is he? Why is he watching her? What is she doing?

Think about a time you felt as if you were being watched. What did it feel like?

853. Your heroine is finally ready to get married – almost. Before she begins her husband hunt, she's decided to head to a tropical island for one last fling.

Where does she go?

Who does she meet and how steamy does her last fling get?

What happens when her vacation is over?

854. Your heroine, a romance review writer, is tired of reading about romance. She wants one of her own.

Trouble is, none of the men she meets come close to the men on the pages of her romance novels.

When a wish upon a star comes true, she realizes she may have wished for more than she can handle. What happens?

855. When your heroine, an interior designer, lands the job of her dreams – redesigning the mansion of a renowned businessman – she's in for more than she bargained for.

While he's given her free rein to design her home, he wants her to live with him for a month so she can get a feel for his personality, his lifestyle and his tastes.

How bad does she want the job? Bad enough to agree to move in with him.

And while she's confident in her ability to design the perfect home for him, she's not so confident she can keep her hands off of him or her libido in check for a full month of close quarters.

What happens?

How does she manage to live with this rich hottie without sleeping with him, or does she?

Want to add a paranormal twist? Make the hottie a vampire or other unnatural creature and amplify the heat and the danger.

856. Your heroine has struggled with her weight her entire life. Finally, she's lost the weight she wants and feels good about her body.

She feels good, good enough to take an exotic vacation with the single goal to find a man to appreciate her body from head to toe, and maybe back again!

However she gets more than she bargains for when she meets a delicious man on vacation who also has a past he'd rather forget and some issues of his own. Who does she meet? What are his issues? What does she learn about herself?

857. Your heroine, a personal shopper and stylist, spends her days dressing and shopping for women.

Rarely does a man walk through her doors, yet when your hero requests her services she's in for more than a day at the mall.

Why does he need her styling help and what happens when they meet?

858. Your heroine is an athlete and the biggest competition of her life is coming up. Unfortunately, she just broke her leg and won't be able to compete. It's a life changing injury and she's sinking into a depression.

To get her out of her depression her friends send over a male stripper. As the music starts and your heroine enters the room the mood suddenly becomes more awkward than anyone could imagine – the male stripper is......

Who is he and how does your heroine know him? How does this moment change her life and her outlook?

859. Your heroine is dodging a terrible snowstorm. She finds the cabin and decides to take shelter there until the storm passes. She finds herself amidst a man's weekend. What happens next? Are they happy to see her? Disgruntled? Does she feel threatened? If you write erotic romance this is certainly fodder for a kinky scene or two.

860. Love a man in uniform? Your heroine catches your hero taking off his uniform. Is your heroine in the men's locker room accidentally? Intentionally? Have fun!

861. Your heroine is a waitress at a country club. Working a rowdy birthday party for a 45 year old female member, she is aggravated to find out they've hired a stripper, but when he walks through the door it's all she can do to keep her

eyes off him. Will an average night of work turn into the most passionate night of her life? What happens?

862. Judy has a hang-up about her curves. She cannot believe that your hero, a real hottie, would ever be into a girl like her. What does he do that finally convinces her that she's the one he wants?

863. Your heroine is playing games and trying to get the attention of her delinquent and inattentive boyfriend. She begins flirting with a guy. He plays along for a while, long enough to pique her interest, then he calls her on her games. What happens next?

864. A whitewater rafting trip turns into a survival story. Your heroine gets tossed overboard and wakes up downstream. She finds her way to a cabin, but it's occupied by someone. Who? How does he react to his waterlogged intruder?

865. Your heroine has had the week from hell. She's celebrating surviving it by wearing her most comfortable sweats and pigging out on pepperoni pizza, ice cream and chips. She's in slovenly heaven when someone knocks on the door. Who is at the door and what does the gorgeous guy want?

866. Your heroine is on a solitary vacation. She's just emerged from a sauna sans clothes to take a plunge in the snow. She's feeling wild and carefree, and acting just a bit silly. What does she do when she realizes she's being watched? Who is watching her?

867. Your protagonist hears strange noises coming from the other side of a door. They peer through the keyhole. What do they see?

868. It's Leap Day and nothing you do counts. What does your heroine do?

869. Your heroine is at a corporate training retreat. It's being led by a ridiculous, albeit cute, man who is saying things like, "An empty bag cannot stand upright." Surely he cannot be that square. She decides to find out. What does she do?

870. Your heroine wakes from a strange dream. As she heads to work and looks around she realizes her dream is coming true. That night it happens again. Your heroine's dreams are turning into reality. When she dreams of a sexy man and meets him the next day, what happens?

871. Your heroine owns a restaurant. Her chef mouths off at her and to save face in front of the other employees she has to fire him. Later that night she's at a bar and she sees him. He has been drinking. She feels badly and ....what happens?

872. Two bloggers meet at a blogging convention. They hook up and then a misunderstanding keeps them apart. One year later they're surprised to find out they're both hosting the same television show. They hate each other immediately because of the misunderstanding. What happens?

873. On a whitewater rafting trip your heroine and her girlfriends meet up, accidentally, with a boat full of men. What happens?

874. Your heroine is at a bachelorette party with her sister. Her sister gets arrested for getting carried away at a strip club. Your heroine heads to the police station to bail her out and meets a sexy police officer.

875. Your hero is at an interview and he's pretty sure his interviewer is flirting with him. He sure hopes so because she's the woman of his dreams. What happens next?

876. Your heroine is sitting over a blank piece of paper. She's holding a pen in her hand. The wish she writes down will come true and she's trying to figure out exactly what to write down. What does she write?

877. Your heroine accuses a co-worker of stealing something from her. Turns out, she was wrong. She apologizes and he asks her to make up for it by....what does he ask her to do?

878. Your heroine is out on the town with friends. They all leave with someone and she's left alone. What does she do?

879. Your heroine is sitting at the bar with her date. His brother walks in (she's dated him too) the two start fighting over her. What does she do?

880. Your heroine is in the elevator when it breaks. She's with two or three other passengers, one who is extremely good looking. What happens?

881. Your heroine wakes up in the morning, in her bed, fully clothed except for one thing…she's missing a shoe. She cannot find her shoe and she doesn't remember last night.

She returns at the end of the work day to find her missing shoe sitting in front of her door. There's a phone number written on the bottom of the shoe. Does she call it?

882. Your hero wakes up next hung over and naked to his best friend (male or female, you decide). Did they or didn't they? What happens next?

883. Your hero owns a small hotel. He has one guest, a quiet and mysterious woman, for the night. A blizzard has locked them in for a few days – what happens?

884. Your heroine runs a bordello and while she's not innocent, she's never been paid for sex or had sex with a client. Your hero walks in and sets his sights on her. He won't take no for an answer. Why does he want her? Does he have a hidden agenda? How does he try to seduce her and what is her reaction?

885. Your heroine is writing a book about the escapades of the area's richest bachelors. She goes undercover and discovers…

886. Your heroine is in a traveling show. The lead in the main act is injured. This puts her on stage front and center and into the arms of…

887. Little Shop of Pleasures – Your heroine owns an online sex toy store. She's never had any problems and enjoys her job, but now someone is following her. Is it a delightful man of mystery or a dark man with deadly intent?

888. What on earth could a motorcycle gang member and an elementary school librarian have in common? They meet when your librarian's car has a flat tire and he stops to help her repair it.

889. Your heroine/hero takes shelter in a barn only to be surprised in the middle of the night by the owner. What happens?

890. Your hero, a new food blogger/writer for a magazine, pans a bakery café. Your heroine, the owner, has a bone to pick with him. She tracks him down and...

891. Your hero knocks on his neighbor's door. Your heroine mistakes him for the handyman she called. Without correcting her, he makes the repairs, then asks to borrow some sugar.

892. Your hero and heroine made an agreement. If neither one of them were married by the time they were 30, they'd hook up. It's the night of your heroine's 30th birthday, she's single and your hero is knocking on her door.

893. Your hero catches your heroine stealing something from him. What's her punishment?

894. Your heroine is kidnapped and given as a sexual toy to your hero. What happens?

895. Your heroine believes she is showing up to volunteer to help a blind man. Your hero lets her continue to believe he's blind. What happens?

896. Your heroine owns a club where her magic causes patrons to feel euphoric. Alas, her magic doesn't have the same effect on her – until she meets a man with his own magic.

897. Your hero is on the run and hiding. He takes a job as a resident handyman and finds he has trouble resisting the establishment's owner.

898. Your heroine shows up at a masquerade ball and is mistaken for someone else – someone who apparently has a voracious sexual appetite. What happens?

899. Your hero stows away on a ship. Your heroine finds him and helps hide him. What happens?

900. Your heroine takes a wilderness survival course in rugged Alaska and learns about more than survival from her guide.

901. Your heroine wants to hire an assassin to kill the person who murdered her family. She'll do anything to convince him.

902. Your heroine is a shifter and part of a dying breed. She may be the last person who can carry on their species, but more than one man wants to take her and make her his.

903. Your heroine sacrificed her reputation to save another. Tired of all the whispers and gossip behind her back she's decided to earn her reputation. How?

904. Your heroine owns an amusement park. One night she finds two men hanging out in her paintball room. What happens?

905. Your hero is getting ready to marry. Despite his reputation, he has zero experience and wants to impress his soon to be wife. He hires a courtesan to teach him.

906. Your heroine is an inventor and she needs someone to help her test her new invention.

907. Your heroine and her friends decide to take a trip to a dude ranch, but her friends bail at the last minute leaving your heroine alone with cowboys for a week.

908. Your hero has wanted your heroine for years. He is surprised when she shows up at his front door.

909. Your hero is heading out on a mission that will probably get him killed. Before he goes there's just one thing he wants to do, spend one long night with your heroine.

910. Your heroine is out on her sailboat when the boat starts taking on water. She flags down another boat and finds that two men are on board. What happens?

911. Your heroine finds a pair of shoes that she just can't resist. She puts them on and...

912. Your hero is trapped in a future where women are the citizens and the men are the slaves. He's chosen to become "trained" and serve the queen. What happens?

913. Your heroine is a historian. Her favorite time period is the middle ages. She believes she's having one of her favorite dreams, one with a knight in shining armor and a roll in the hay, but this time it isn't a dream.

914. When your heroine was a teenager she took a dare. It was a moment she never forgot. Apparently neither did he. Ten years later, at a chance meeting, the heat still blazes between them.

915. Your heroine writes fairy tales for children. She never expects to see a real fairy show up in her home or in her bed.

916. Your heroine, a vampire, has been assigned to watch a lone vampire who has just entered her maker's territory. She's sworn to protect her maker, but she's drawn to the lone vampire. Why is he there? What happens?

917. Your hero is psychic. Your heroine is a police detective. She's skeptical that he can do anything more than get in the way. He's tired of proving himself to cynical cops. What happens when they're on a stakeout?

918. Your heroine and two co-workers get locked in a closet during a work party. What happens?

919. Your hero is on a quest to recover a stolen family artifact. What happens when she meets the thief?

920. Your heroine's husband cheated on her in a very public way. She's given up men until she meets your hero and he shows her that she is worthy of devoted love and passion.

921. Your heroine has just received a fatal diagnosis. She decides to have one last adventure before she goes. Where does she go and what does she do?

922. Your heroine walks into a brothel looking for the man that killed her dad. He's known to hang out there. In order to find him, and have her vengeance, she becomes an employee. What happens?

923. While walking through an antique store, your heroine finds a box. Just touching it sends tingles through her body. What happens when she opens the box?

924. Your hero is sent to infiltrate a rival family's business. His job...to seduce the owner's daughter. What happens?

925. Your heroine is tending to a grief stricken man. She's a healer. How does she heal him? Why is he grief stricken?

926. Your hero owns a ranching business. A representative from a local oil and gas company wants to buy his land.

He's not selling, but he's willing to let her try to convince him.

Notes:

_____
_____
_____
_____
_____
_____
_____
_____
_____
_____
_____
_____
_____
_____
_____
_____
_____
_____
_____
_____
_____
_____
_____
_____

Chapter 9

Write It Backwards

927. It's Christmas and this story starter can take many paths. Consider starting it with a woman hiking on Christmas morning with her dogs. Maybe she meets a man who needs help. Or maybe your story ends up here with two people on a special holiday hike. How did they end up here? Write your story backwards.

928. Your story ends with your heroine opening the door and seeing your hero's face.

929. Your story ends with a bar full of people standing up and applauding. Why?

930. Your story ends with your heroine opening a box and finding her heart's desire inside. What is it? How did she get here?

931. Your story ends with your heroine slapping your hero on the, t. It's a private joke they share.

932. Your hero is being embraced by your hero's mother. It's a huge moment. Why?

933. Your hero and heroine collapse in exhaustion. Why?

934. Your heroine is climbing out of a hot bubble bath and your hero is waiting with a towel. How'd they get here? Where are they?

935. Your hero is walking down the street at night. It's raining and he's whistling.

936. Your heroine puts on her bright red trench coat and heads out the door.

937. Your heroine wraps her fingers around a locket that is hanging from a chain around her neck.

938. Your heroine claps her hands together and her dog comes running toward her.

939. End your story with, "He kissed me."

940. End your story with, "Do you really want to chance it?"

941. End your story with, "Be safe on your way."

942. End your story with, "I headed over in his direction."

943. End your story with, "Whiskey, please."

944. Your heroine is being propositioned in a bar. She challenges the person with a threat. The person looks deep into her eyes and backs off. Why? What brought her to this bar? Where is your hero?

945. Your story ends in a court room with people rejoicing and people wailing. What side are your hero and heroine on? What has just happened? How did they get here?

946. Your heroine is stepping out from the cold into the bright warm sunshine. She drops a winter coat from her shoulders. Where is she? How did she get here?

947. Your hero is cleaning his weapon and putting it away. Your heroine is standing behind him. What is his weapon and why does it need cleaning? What happened?

948. Your heroine is giving your hero a ring. Why? What does the ring symbolize?

949. End your story with, "He/She leapt into the carriage and the horses clattered off down the street."

950. End your story with, "I wish I had as much faith in myself as you have in me."

951. End your story with, Speaker #1 "Was it worth it? The sacrifice you had to make to find out the truth of your past?" Speaker #2 He/she exhaled, unclenched his/her fists and nodded. "Yes."

952. End your story with, "I glanced up at the shimmering snowflakes that softly drifted toward my face.

953. End your story with, Speaker #1 "Where will this take us?" Speaker #2 "Wherever you want it to."

954. End your story with, "Welcome to the end of the world."

955. End your story with, "It was nice to finally peel that big red bull's eye off of my back."

956. End your story with, "Everything has changed."

957. End your story with, Speaker #1 "You're not going to punish me?" Speaker #2 "I didn't say that."

958. End your story with, "I'm glad we agree on something."

959. Your hero and heroine are shaking hands. Why? What are they agreeing on?

960. End your story with, "She held onto him with everything she had."

961. End your story with, "She wondered if she'd ever see her home again."

962. End your story with, "He holds my hand and I wonder if I'll ever be brave enough to let it go."

963. End your story with, Speaker #1 "What did you tell them?" Speaker #2 "You'll never know."

964. A large barn is burning. Flames are reaching for the nighttime stars. Smoke stretches toward the sky. Your hero and heroine stand together watching it burn. How'd they get here? What happened?

965. Your heroine kisses a small child on the nose. Her heart is full of joy and contentment. Who is the child? How did your heroine get to this point?

966. Your heroine stands before a large gift. Who gave it to her? What does it mean?

967. Your hero opens a letter. What does the letter say? Who is it from? Why did he get the letter? What brought him to this point?

968. End your story with, "She drove through the car wash one last time. As the blower blew away the last drop of water on her windshield, she let him go."

969. End your story with, "He watched her in the kitchen, wearing nothing but his shirt, and knew with every cell in his body that he'd made the right decision."

970. End your story with, "Can I dance with the bride?"

971. End your story with, "Thank you for the cookie."

972. End your story with, Speaker #1 "Did you win?" Speaker #2 "I'm here aren't I?"

973. End your story with, "It was a dark and stormy night."

974. Your hero and heroine close the door to their home, sit down on the couch and fall asleep. What happened to bring them to this point?

975. Your heroine swings her fist and punches someone. She walks away feeling tremendously satisfied. How'd she get to this point? Who did she punch?

976. End your story with, "You, my dear, are a wise woman."

977. Your heroine finishes her beer, or glass of wine, sets it down on the bar, and grabs the hand of the man next to her and they walk out of the bar hand in hand.

978. Your heroine jumps from the top of a cliff into the deep water below. Your hero follows after her. Where are they and why are they there?

979. Your hero and heroine stumble on a dead body in a horse stable. Where are they and how did they end up in a horse stable?

980. Your hero and heroine walk back into the house where they met.

981. Your hero brings your heroine back to life. Your story ends when her heart starts beating again and she smiles up at him.

982. Your heroine claps her hands together to dust the dirt off them. She smiles, turns, and walks down the street.

983. Your heroine is receiving an award. She looks into the audience and sees the people she loves. What award is she receiving? Who is in the audience?

984. Your hero and heroine stand atop a mountain, looking at the water below them. Where are they? How'd they get there?

985. Your hero kicks back his feet. He's sitting on the beach. Readers presume he is alone. He's not. Your heroine is there. She walks up and hands him something cold to drink.

986. Your heroine has just made the biggest choice of her life. She's back where she belongs. Looking at the results of her decision, she's feeling satisfied.

987. Your heroine looks in the mirror and finally likes what she sees.

988. End your story with, "She put the last item in her suitcase and closed the lid."

989. It's New Year's Eve and your heroine is remembering where she was one year ago today. She turns to your hero and he mouths the words "I love you," from across the room.

990. Your hero is walking across hot coals to show his love and devotion. Just before he steps on the coals, your heroine agrees to marry him. He's so happy he walks to her and doesn't realize he's stepped on the coals.

991. Your hero and heroine are renewing their vows.

992. Your hero is hanging up his uniform and awards. He's putting them away in the closet. Turning around, he sees his future – your heroine.

993. Your hero and heroine are at a double wedding.

994. Your hero grabs your heroine's cell phone and throws it out the car window as they drive away.

995. Your hero brings your heroine a puppy. She's pleased, but pretends to be slightly put out that she'll have to care for it. What brought them to this point?

996. Your hero and heroine are sitting in the dark. The power just went out and they don't mind a bit.

997. Your heroine is standing behind a bar. She pours a drink for a patron, looks up from the bar and sees your hero standing in the doorway.

998. Your story ends with your hero and heroine having a picnic in the countryside.

999. Your hero and heroine both yell, "go away" at the person knocking on their door. They fall back into bed and under the covers.

1000. Your heroine is standing in the turret of a castle looking down at the countryside around her. She sees your hero riding up on his horse and her body is filled with relief. She runs out to greet him. They kiss and live Happily Ever After.

1001. Your heroine is crying. Why? Are they tears of joy? Sadness? Relief? Anger?

~~******~~

Note To Readers

Thank you.

I'd like to thank you from the bottom of my heart. I sincerely hope that you enjoyed 1001 Romance Story Starters and I look forward to hearing about your success.

When you publish your story, send me a link and I'll announce it on my blog.

In the meantime, to help you get to the point of publication – visit http://makealivingwritingromance.com/worksheets-and-free-downloads and take advantage of the free resources including the "Turn your idea into a novel" worksheet.

Thanks again and happy writing!

Annette Elton

About The Author

As a child, I remember spending countless hours hanging out in my father's airplane hangar. There's not much for a little girl to do there so I relied on my imagination. I'd lie on the ground outside the hangar - the scent of motor oil and fresh grass mixing into a beloved concoction that's still an oddly comforting scent to me today – and I'd daydream.

I'd make up stories. Leaves came alive and shared their tales. Mice would go on epic adventures. And as I grew, so did my characters – eventually my penchant for storytelling evolved into a love for romance and romantic fiction.

Today, I have more ideas than I know what to do with. I've been a professional book reviewer for a national magazine, a published author and ghostwriter, and a business owner.

I feel tremendously fortunate that I have been able to hold onto my penchant for daydreaming and am delighted to share some of my many story ideas with others.

Remember, if you'd like to spice up your writing or need a little help, you can find free tools and resources just waiting for you at www.MakeaLivingWritingRomance.com. Stop by and say "hi"!

CPSIA information can be obtained
at www.ICGtesting.com
Printed in the USA
BVOW04s0726050317
477784BV00017B/1008/P